A Dictionary of Doctrinal Terms

Fisher Humphreys•Philip Wise

BROADMAN PRESS
Nashville, Tennessee

To
Caroline
and
Cynthia

© Copyright 1983 • Broadman Press
All rights reserved.
4211-41
ISBN: 0-8054-1141-0
Dewey Decimal Classification: 230.03
Subject Heading: THEOLOGY—DICTIONARIES
Library of Congress Catalog Card Number: 81-86635
Printed in the United States of America

Preface

Our primary purpose in writing this dictionary is to provide a resource for Christian ministers who are preparing to preach or to teach about theological subjects. We have written for the church generally rather than for the church's scholars, though we hope there would be no reason to be ashamed if a scholar should happen to read the book.

We have selected one hundred terms, all in current use in evangelical churches in the United States. We avoided the names of modern movements and trends, such as *dispensationalism* and *liberation theology*, and dealt instead with those terms which the contemporary church has inherited from the past but found it necessary to retain for its own use. If our selection has been successful, these are one hundred of the most important terms which the contemporary Christian community uses to formulate and communicate its faith.

Most of the essays include a brief definition followed by selected, representative observations on the biblical usage of the terms. This is followed, when it is pertinent, by an even briefer summary of important changes in the usage of the term in church history. In virtually every entry, an effort is made to analyze the term, sometimes to clear up confusion in its usage. We also have felt at liberty frequently to inject insights of our own into the book when we felt that readers might find them useful.

The son of one of us once asked his father to explain the difference between a dictionary and an encyclopedia, and he received this response. Whereas a dictionary is about words, an encyclopedia is about the things to which the words refer. With this common sense distinction in mind, we confess to our readers that this book is not exactly one or the other. Like a dictionary, it includes discussions of the terms. Like an encyclopedia, it includes discussions of the realities also. The thirty-third entry, for example, is about *God*, the term; but it also is about God, the One to whom the term refers. For obvious reasons, our deepest concern is for the latter.

We trust this book will be read as a seamless unity. We divided the work, but each of us rewrote the work of the other, and we are in basic agreement about all the entries. This was easy for us because we share a common theological outlook as well as a common Christian faith. Both of us accept responsibility for the entire work, and no responsibility is to be attributed to our editors or publishers or to our fine secretaries, Mrs. Dianne Parrish and Mrs. Hildred Stewart.

The audience for our book is the Christian community. One of us is a pastor, the other a seminary professor. We hope that our effort to bridge the gap between our two ministries will make the book a good resource for ministers of all kinds.

Contents

A

AGE OF ACCOUNTABILITY. The age at which a child is responsible to God for his own behavior and decisions.

The Bible contains no mention of the age of accountability. The church has created this phrase in recognition of the fact that infants are not responsible for their actions, and adults are responsible for theirs. This teaching is consistent with the biblical revelation.

Also called the *age of reason,* this concept may be traced to the Jewish practice of bar mitzvah, or the ceremony at which a Jewish boy of about thirteen years of age is recognized as an adult.

Determining when a child becomes responsible for his actions is difficult. Many factors contribute to a child's reaching this stage, including parental guidance, the child's own sensitivity, exposure to moral and religious instruction.

It is agreed generally that prior to the age of accountability, a child is not held responsible for his sin. If he should die before the age of accountability, he would be received into God's presence, as a result of Christ's saving work.

Two extremes must be avoided in determining a child's receptivity to the gospel message. On the one hand, the child should not be coerced to make a decision he does not understand. On the other hand, the child should not be discouraged if he or she shows an unusual religious sensitivity at a very early age.

APOLOGETICS. The part of evangelism which works to help

make faith in Jesus Christ possible for people who have intellectual difficulties with the Christian message.

People experience various barriers to Christian faith. Some do not have faith because they have never been told the story of Christ. Some have heard the story but have misunderstood it. Some simply do not want to be Christians. Evangelism is the effort to help these people trust in Christ. When the barrier to belief is intellectual, apologetics is the proper form of evangelism.

The two biggest intellectual barriers to belief are evidence and suffering. People cannot see God; how can they be sure that he is real? There have been many religious leaders; what evidence is there that Jesus Christ is the true one? Again, so many relatively innocent people suffer pointlessly, such as children with horrible diseases or in war-torn communities. Why does God let this happen? These are the kinds of questions which an apologist must try to answer.

The traditional definition of *apologetics* is "defense of the faith." There are two problems with this definition. One is that it implies that we are to try to win arguments, whereas the greatest apologists of the church have been more concerned to win men than to win arguments. The other problem is that this definition suggests that the Christian must be on the defensive, when in fact the apologist often needs to take the offensive role, pointing out the problems of unbelief.

Christian apologists carry out their work in various ways. Sometimes they attempt to defend the existence of God by using philosophical arguments. They may use cultural apologetics, pointing to artists and others whose vision confirms aspects of Christian teaching, such as human sinfulness or human yearning for immortality. They may use historical apologetics to defend the reality of Jesus Christ, even the reality of his resurrection. How, they may ask, can you account for the existence of the church if Christ is not risen? Again, they may take the offensive against idolatry (do you worship money, power, or fame?), or against atheism (how do you know there is no God?), or against agnosticism (how do you know that no one can know if there is a

God?). They may use religious experience, their own and that of other Christians, to confirm the relevance of faith in our time. Or they may resort to an apologetics of explanation, simply putting the Christian message in clear words, because what many people have rejected is not actually the Christian message, but a misunderstanding of it.

Some Christians disapprove of apologetics. They insist that the gospel needs only to be proclaimed, not to be defended. While this is an understandable position, how does one respond to a person who says: "I see what you are talking about, and it's a wonderful message, but why should I believe it?" The number of occasions when one may need to do apologetics may be few, but if help is available for those who want to believe but find it difficult, then help should be given. "Always be prepared to make a defense to any one who calls you to account for the hope that is in you, yet do it with gentleness" (1 Pet. 3:15).

ATONEMENT. The work which Christ carried out by his suffering, death, and resurrection.

Although it is not certain, it is probable that the root meaning of *atonement* is reconciliation; to atone is to "at-one," to bring together quarreling parties. Reconciliation is one of the ways in which Christ's work was understood in the early church: "God was in Christ, reconciling the world unto himself" (2 Cor. 5:19, KJV). Other understandings of the work of Christ include justification (Rom. 3:22-26), redemption, and forgiveness (Eph. 1:7).

A theory of atonement is an interpretation of the meaning of Jesus' passion, death, and resurrection, which makes clear how those events make it possible for sinners to be forgiven, redeemed, and so on. While some Christians do not like theories of the atonement, many Christians find them helpful to try to understand how Jesus' work provided salvation. They point out that the Bible contains a number of explanations of Christ's work. The most fully developed one is the idea of sacrifice (see Heb. 9:1 to 10:25), but there are many others.

The most influential theory of atonement in the Protestant

churches has been that of John Calvin, which is called the theory of substitutionary punishment. The idea is a simple and powerful one: Christ took the punishment due to sinners so that sinners might be forgiven. More recently, a theory held by Swedish theologian Gustaf Aulen has been found helpful: Christ engaged all the forces of darkness and evil in a mighty battle, and by his death and resurrection he defeated them and set humanity free from them. A third theory which many Christians in the twentieth century have found helpful might be called costly forgiveness: just as parents, for example, may have to suffer in order to forgive rebellious children, so God in Christ suffered the most outrageous consequences of human sin in order to forgive sinners.

The work which Christ did is a unique, divine work; there is no exact human analogy for it and, therefore, no complete explanation of it. Perhaps that is why the Bible contains a number of different ways of speaking of it. The church must continue to draw upon all the biblical expressions in order to clarify what it means when it proclaims that "Christ died for our sins" (1 Cor. 15:3).

AUTHORITY. The right to judge, control, influence, or be believed.

Christians believe that all authority resides in God (Rom. 13:1), and all other authority is derived. Since Jesus Christ is God's ultimate revelation of himself, Christ is the final arbiter of all derived authority (Matt. 28:18).

The Bible is authoritative for faith and practice for the following reasons: God inspired the Scriptures; the Scriptures witness to God's self-disclosure in history; and the Scriptures serve as a medium for God's self-expression today. The Bible has authority second only to Christ.

The church also has a derived authority. It is not the authority to judge but to influence. The church is authorized and empowered by Christ to proclaim the gospel. Baptists speak of the authority of the local church, meaning the right of a single congregation under God to make its own decisions.

Pastoral authority is similar to the authority of the church. It is not the power to demand, but the privilege to serve (1 Tim. 3:1). The pastor's authority is derived from his task, which is to proclaim the good news of Jesus Christ (1 Tim. 4:13). There is no biblical justification for a pastoral dictatorship within the church.

The Bible also recognizes civil government as a legitimate, though unredeemed, source of derived authority (Rom. 13:1 *ff*.). Christians are to obey the civil authorities (Titus 3:1).

Two other sources of authority in the church ought to be mentioned. There is an authority of scholarship which should be respected. Those who study and reflect on the Scriptures earn the right to speak with limited authority. Also, there is a derived sense of authority which comes through religious experience. One's personal experience with God carries with it an inner conviction which is authoritative for the individual, provided the experience is consistent with the gospel.

B

BAPTISM. The act of initiation into the Christian faith.

Cleansing was a ritual act of religious purification for the Jews. John the Baptist adapted this ritual of water purification as a symbol of national repentance (Mark 1:4; Luke 3:7). Jesus acknowledged the validity of John's baptism by submitting himself as a candidate. There is no record of Jesus having baptized anyone, but he encouraged his disciples to baptize in the name of the Father, Son, and Holy Spirit (Matt. 28:19).

Baptism is recognized by Baptists as one of the two ordinances which Jesus instituted. It is like the Lord's Supper in that it is for believers only and in that it proclaims Christ's sacrificial death. It is unique in that it is an unrepeatable act. The biblical method of baptism was immersion.

As a symbol, baptism works at three levels. It is a sermon which reminds believers of Christ's death, burial, and resurrection. For the candidate it is an act of obedience to Christ's command, and also a symbol of his desire to renounce sin and live in the power of the Holy Spirit. For the church, it is an act of obedience by which new Christians are admitted into the fellowship of faith.

BIBLE. The sixty-six books of the Old and New Testaments which together constitute the Christian Scriptures.

The books, which include several kinds of literature (history, aphorisms, songs, parables, letters, and so on), were written over a period of many centuries by various persons. Collections of the books were made first by the Jews and later by the church. The process of determining the books to be included in the Bible was called canonization; some disagreement existed and still exists concerning the canon (some churches include the books known as the Apocrypha in addition to the sixty-six books of the Old and New Testaments).

The process of canonization was a mysterious one. Scholars surmise that the church attempted to include books which were widely accepted by the Jewish community as Scripture plus those which were deemed to be apostolic and, therefore, authoritative in their presentation of the Christian revelation. The twenty-seven books of the New Testament were first listed in a letter of Athanasius (AD 367) and soon thereafter listed by councils at Rome (AD 382) and Carthage (AD 397).

Though awareness of the process of canonization seems to some to undermine confidence in the revelatory character of the Bible, it need not do so. It is perfectly consistent that God would inspire men to write the books of the Bible, direct his people to collect these books into a canon, assist his people to transmit Scripture from one generation to the next and to translate it into many languages, and then illuminate those who hear and read the Bible to understand its message.

Though it is a large collection of diverse texts, the Bible exhibits a high degree of unity, for it speaks of one personal, transcendent, Creator, God who acted in the history of Israel and participated in the story of Jesus Christ to redeem the world and create a community of faith.

Even by human standards the Bible is a remarkable book. It has for many centuries been the most widely-distributed and frequently-translated book in the world. The beauty of its language and the influence it has exerted over civilization have no equal in literature.

But these qualities do not exhaust the importance of the Bible, for Christian faith believes that the authority of Scripture is divine rather than merely human. The Bible not only records persons' experiences with God; it also records God's gracious revelation of himself to persons. The Bible, therefore, should be read as the Word of God. When it is read in this way, the reader finds himself spoken to—addressed—by God himself.

Though the church universally accepts the Bible as God's Word, disputes exist in the church concerning the authority of the Bible. For example, is the Bible a unique authority, or is church tradition a second source of revelation? Did God inspire the words of the Bible or only its thoughts or, perhaps, its stories or its symbols or images? Is the Bible itself a revelation of God or a record of revelations which God gave at different times, or both? Is the Bible inerrant in the details it mentions incidentally, or is its truth located rather in its great message of God and his gracious acts of salvation? Does the authority of the Bible reside only in the original manuscripts—the so-called autographs, which no longer exist—or is its authority transmitted to modern texts and translations? Does reverence for the Bible entail a willingness to study the Bible analytically, or does it preclude such study? Can a Christian have too much reverence for the Bible and commit bibliolatry (making an idol of the Bible)? What principles should be followed in order to interpret the Bible (hermeneutics)? These and other questions are likely to continue to be debated in the church in the future as they have in the past. Meanwhile, faithful Christians continue to read the Bible, study it, teach it, live by it, and proclaim its message to the world.

Christianity is not the only religion to have a holy book. Islam has its Koran and Hinduism its Vedas. The church will always live by its Bible. In one sense the church is more fundamental than the Bible, for the church existed before the Bible. But in another sense the Bible is more fundamental than the church, for the church over the centuries has been shaped and directed by the message of the Scriptures. The Holy Spirit who first inspired the writing of the Bible continues to guide the church to understand and appropriate the message of the Bible as its final authority on earth for faith and life.

C

CHRISTIAN. Either a person who has personal faith in Jesus Christ; or a person, action, or institution which exhibits certain moral qualities, such as love, which are associated with Jesus Christ.

The ambiguity of these two usages leads to confusion. How is a person to answer the question, "Are you a Christian?" If the question is understood to refer to personal faith, he may answer simply, "Yes. I believe in Christ." But if he understands the question to refer to moral qualities, he may answer, "I am not as Christian as I should be."

Both usages of the term are now widespread, and it is pointless to insist that one has priority over the other. What matters is that we recognize the distinction. No moral qualities, however Christian, are a substitute for personal faith in Jesus Christ. On the other hand, the importance of and need for faith in Christ should not prevent one from appreciating the moral impact which Jesus Christ has made upon culture and society, even those aspects of culture and society which do not confess faith in Christ.

CHURCH. The worldwide community of persons who have faith in Jesus Christ. This community of faith may be said to be present in a particular location (1 Cor. 1:2). The word for *church* in the New Testament *(ekklesia)*, like the Hebrew word it often translated *(Qahal)*, has a root meaning of assembly. Therefore, the New Testament can speak of several churches (Acts 15:14).

The Bible reveals that religious faith is a social matter and that God has always been actively creating a community of faith. In the Old Testament, this was the people of Israel; in the New Testament, it was the church, which is the new Israel (Gal. 6:16). The Book of Acts tells the story of the young church struggling, with the guidance of the Spirit, to receive into the community people other than Jews: Samaritans, God-fearers, and Gentiles. In doing this, it was following the example of Jesus, who called a motley group of men to be his disciples and who had the reputation, unsavory among Pharisees and others, of being a friend of publicans and sinners.

The New Testament uses numerous metaphors to picture the church, such as vine and branches (John 15), holy nation (1 Pet. 2:9), and body of Christ (Rom. 12:4-8)—the most fully developed of the metaphors. Throughout history the church has sought to express its identity in various ways, one of the best known of which is the four notes of the church expressed in the Nicene Creed, the "one Holy Catholic and Apostolic Church." In the twentieth century, the ecumenical movement stimulated thinking about the church's nature. As a result, some theologians now speak of the church as a dynamic event rather than a static thing; and others argue that the church does not have a mission; rather, the church is a mission.

One continuing temptation has been for the church to think of itself as an institution rather than as a community. In this debate, the extreme positions are for institutional concerns— such as programs, organizations, budgets, and properties—to be valued at the expense of persons or for concern for persons to lead to the renouncing of all institutional forms. The latter cannot really be done, for what happens is that an institutional structure is accepted unawares, which can be more tyrannical than one which is openly acknowledged.

Another temptation, especially in the modern world of political democracies, has been for Christians to regard faith as an individualistic matter. While it is true that faith is intimate and personal, solitary religion is not biblical. Commitment to

God's people is entailed in faith. The community is as fundamental a reality as the individual.

CHURCH AND STATE. The relationship between the Christian community and the political establishment which governs a nation.

Before the formation of the United States, it was widely assumed in European nations and in smaller political entities that religion was part of the culture which bound a people together. A ruler was thought to have a moral and spiritual obligation to establish, that is, formally support in various ways including funding through taxation, the religion of which he was an adherent. From approximately the time of the Roman Emperor Constantine (fourth century) until the Reformation (sixteenth century), the established religion of Europe was Christianity. Rulers were key figures in the establishment of Protestant churches as well as the Roman Catholic Church after the Reformation. The establishment of religion in various states meant that religious liberty was rare and, where it existed, it was limited to bare toleration.

The United States was the first nation established without an official religion. It was established with a Bill of Rights which assures its citizens that no government effort would be made to control, support, or suppress religious faith and practice. In a sense this assurance of liberty represented an act of faith on the part of Thomas Jefferson and the other Founding Fathers, for no precedent existed which could demonstrate the viability of a nation without a religious establishment.

The separation of church and state in America has never been total. Chaplains minister in the armed forces and in the Congress. "In God We Trust" is engraved on coins, elected officials are sworn into office with their hands on Bibles, and so on. Whatever decisions are made about these and other matters, a fundamental difference in the relation of church and state exists between America and nations with an official religion, however democratic and tolerant the latter may be.

Many have feared that without official political support, the church would wither and die. This has proved unfounded. Religion flourishes in the atmosphere of liberty provided by the United States Constitution. Further, since true devotion to God cannot be coerced but must be freely given, the state which provides religious liberty permits its citizens a better opportunity for true religion than the state which establishes religion, however true that religion may be.

But the state which provides religious liberty thereby also allows its citizens to have no religion at all or a false religion. This fact has not always been recognized by the churches. It is the price to be paid in order for people to be free. The responsibility of the Christian church is to evangelize the people of its own land so that they may freely give their allegiance to God. This responsibility is not shared by the state.

How ought a church, committed to religious liberty and to the separation of church and state, participate in national political life? It is not the case that commitment to separation of church and state leads to disinterest in political life. On the negative side, Christians must not seek or accept public moneys (taxes) to support any religious activities. Positively, church members should support, by voting and other active means, laws which protect and promote moral values which the church holds—such as respect for all persons, peace, and justice—but never support laws which coerce religious activities.

The establishment of religion, the withholding of religious liberty, and the social control of the religious practices of a people have been justified in terms of the life of the nation Israel. Religious liberty and freedom of conscience are justified in terms of the biblical teachings against oppression, in terms of the divine origin of the gift of human freedom, in terms of Jesus' call to people to follow him, and in terms of the kind of response—love of God and neighbor—which sums up the Christian practice, a response which is meaningless unless it is freely given.

CHURCH GOVERNMENT. The process by which the community of faith arrives at decisions; the allocation of authority over the life of the community. Also known as church order.

When the early Christian community was formed, neither Jesus nor the apostles provided a detailed plan for the future governance of the community. Understandably, the early church was guided by leaders with personal charisma. Also understandably, some of its early structures were similar to the structure of the Jewish community from which its first members had come, structures such as elders. Probably, various kinds of church government existed in the churches which were established through the missionary activity of Paul and the other apostles.

A familiar analysis of types of government distinguishes oligarchy (authority resides in a self-perpetuating group in the community) from representative government (authority resides in a small elected group in the community), and both from democracy (authority resides in the entire community). The Roman Catholic Church is governed by an oligarchy made up of bishops who alone can ordain other bishops. The Presbyterian churches are governed by elected elders. Baptists are governed by the decisions of the congregation. In general, church governments reflect the kind of civil government which prevailed at the time of their historical beginnings, although a case can be made that the commitment of Christians to participation in congregational decision making enhanced the possibilities of a democracy prevailing in civil government.

Some objections have been raised to this analysis. One is that no churches function solely with any one form. This is true. Thus, the Roman Catholic bishops might pay careful attention to the will of their people, and Baptist churches might delegate great decision-making power to their pastors and to other leaders. Even so, when there is disagreement, the bishops have final authority in the Roman Catholic Church, and the congregation in a Baptist church.

A second objection is that Baptists do not really have a democracy, for they are to arrive at decisions not by voting for what they want, but by voting for what they believe God wants. This is true of all three forms of church government: each is an arrangement to help the church arrive at an understanding of God's will. Some may prefer to call the third form of church government congregational decision making. This is understandable, but the process is democratic rather than representative or oligarchical.

Many Christians are troubled about which of these forms is biblical. In the past, supporters of each view defended their view as the only biblical one. Today it is more widely recognized that the New Testament churches were governed in various ways. If this is accepted, the biblical view today would be to accept the diversity of forms of church government and to be flexible about the form of decision making. Thus, for example, the oligarchy can be appreciated for the efficiency it provides and the democracy for its provision for all Christians to participate in the life of the church.

COMMITMENT. The decision of the Christian to be a faithful follower of Christ.

Though this is not a biblical word, it is a concept which is taught throughout the Bible (see Rom. 12:1-2). Despite the variety of Christian life-styles, there is a consensus among Christians that commitment is a Christian virtue. It is synonymous in the Christian vocabulary with dedication, devotion, fidelity, seriousness, and discipline. A typical example of biblical exhortations to commitment is Jesus' injunction: "No one who puts his hand to the plow and looks back is fit for the kingdom of God" (Luke 9:62).

There is a covenantal aspect to commitment. Since God has been faithful to his word, each believer is expected to be faithful in service and obedience to God.

CONFESSION(S). An acknowledgment of sin; also, statements of faith by an individual Christian or a group of Christians.

Confession is the acknowledgment of wrongdoing and is the first step in repentance. It is followed by the decision to turn away from sin and toward God in an act of true repentance.

Confession of sin may be a private act. As a corporate act of public worship, it is an acknowledgment of the need for forgiveness.

The Old Testament contains a number of references to confession of sin (Ps. 32:5), but only five such usages appear in the New Testament. More often the word *confess* is used in the New Testament to mean the declaration of the truth of something (John 1:20). In this sense, it is a synonym for *profess.*

This usage of the word *confess* was the basis for the statements of faith that have been issued since the Reformation. These have precedents in those Scriptures which record the earliest Christian confession that "Jesus Christ is Lord" (Phil. 2:11). Jesus encouraged this kind of affirmation when he taught, "Everyone who shall confess me before men, him will I also confess before my Father in heaven" (see Matt. 10:32).

The pattern for confessions as statements of faith was set in 1530 with the Lutheran Augsburg Confession. Since that time many Protestant denominations have issued confessions of faith. Baptists have avoided adopting a creed, but from time to time various Baptist groups have adopted statements of faith which expressed the theological consensus of the group. Southern Baptists, for example, adopted in 1925 "The Baptist Faith and Message" and have reaffirmed it a number of times since, most notably in the 1963 revision.

CONSCIENCE. The inner witness which serves as a moral guide to man. It means *co-knowledge.* It is what Chaucer calls "the inwit." Jesus spoke of "the light in you" (Matt. 6:23). James McCracken calls it "the thermometer of the soul."

The Bible teaches that every person has a conscience (Rom. 2:14-15). We are responsible to God; our consciences check on how we fulfill that responsibility (Acts 24:16). One may have a good conscience (1 Tim. 1:5) or a bad conscience (1 Tim. 4:1-2). Conscience may be influenced by God, by moral upbringing, by societal pressures, or by our natural instincts.

Two extremes should be avoided in relation to one's conscience. First, one ought not to injure the conscience of another.

Second, one's conscience ought not to be fettered by the immaturity of another. The conscience is a moral compass which has been injured but not destroyed by sin. It puts us in touch with the moral order of the universe established by God. Christians rely on the Holy Spirit to direct their consciences (Rom. 9:1).

CONVERSION. Changing from one religion or none to Christianity.

The word appears only once in the New Testament (Acts 15:3). Literally, it means to make something out of something else. In the Old Testament, the prophets told the people to turn, return, or turn again, to convert from Baal, from faithfulness, and from backsliding, to God. In the New Testament, John the Baptist sounded the same note, calling on the people to repent. Jesus also called people to repentance.

Three questions arise concerning conversion. First, is conversion real or is it a myth? Jesus taught the reality of the new birth experience which involves a change of mind, emotion, and will (John 3:1-16). The surest demonstration of true conversion is seen in Christians whose life-styles demonstrate the reality of their faith.

Second, does conversion depend on us or does God do it all? This is the issue of predestination and human freedom. If we are not free to convert, then Jesus' injunction to repent and believe is meaningless. True conversion is more than simply saying, "I am sorry." It is an active acceptance of what God has done in Christ. On the other hand, God has taken the initiative to call us to repent, and God graciously accepts those who repent.

Third, is conversion a process or instantaneous? In the sense that there is a time one is not a Christian and another instant in which one is, it is instantaneous. However, it is not necessary for the Christian to be able to pinpoint that instant. The decision to become a Christian often takes place at the end of a long process. What is necessary is to be able to testify that one has made the decision to be a Christian.

CONVICTION OF SIN. The act of being judged guilty; the state of being convinced of one's guilt.

Conviction is not a biblical word but an English word to describe a biblical idea. "The Baptist Faith and Message" uses the word twice, once to affirm that the Holy Spirit convicts of sin and again to point out that new birth comes through the conviction of sin. The Bible teaches that we are judged by God (Rom. 14:10-12). His judgment on us is the fact of our conviction.

Conviction is also a state of being convinced of one's guilt. There is a difference between a jury's verdict and one's own acceptance of personal guilt. Jesus preached repentance, and part of repentance is accepting responsibility for one's sin. This is the inner conviction of sin, and it is a prelude to asking for God's forgiveness.

One question concerning conviction is whether it is the work of the Holy Spirit alone (see John 15:8-11) or whether the preacher should attempt to give conviction by preaching against sin. The tradition of revivalism is that a large part of preaching should be against sin. This has led some to observe that what is preached is often the bad news rather than the good news. On the other hand, it has been observed that in the sermons recorded in Acts, no effort is made to convince people of their sins; the messages there are about what God has done in Christ to rescue sinners. Perhaps the issue is pastoral rather than theological. If the preacher believes that people deep down are denying their need, he may speak of it; but if he judges that they are aware of their need, he may speak positively of how Christ has provided for their need.

COVENANT. The relationship which God graciously establishes with his people, which is summarized in the words: "I . . . will be your God, and you shall be my people" (Lev. 26:12). The covenant relation between God and Israel was at the center of Israel's faith and life, even though Israel often violated the covenant by disobedience.

The idea of a covenant is not inherently religious. Thus, people make business covenants or contracts, and marriage is a covenant or formal agreement.

The use of covenant as a metaphor for the relations between God and God's people involves two risks. One is that religion could be perceived, as many covenants are, as a relationship between two peers for their mutual benefit. The Old Testament avoided this idea by repeatedly insisting that the transcendent, holy God alone established the covenant and that the covenant was gracious and for the benefit of Israel alone, not for the mutual benefit of God and Israel.

The second risk in perceiving Israel's relation with God as a covenant is legalism. The Old Testament avoided this by emphasizing that Israel, in breaking the covenant, not only violated God's rules but also betrayed God himself, personally, and by insisting that people could never stand in a proper relationship with God except by God's initiative and grace.

The early Christians understood Jesus Christ to have created a new covenant with people, by his sacrifice of himself. In a sense the older covenant with Israel was replaced, and in another sense it was fulfilled in the creation of the new community of faith called the church. The old covenant had been written in stone (the Ten Commandments); the new was written on human hearts. The old was for national Israel; the new was through Israel for the world. The old was sealed by the blood of animals; the new was sealed by the blood of Christ (see Jer. 31:31-34; Matt. 26:26-29; Heb. 9:1-28).

In the history of Christian thought, the word *covenant* has also played other more specialized roles. In Protestant theology, it distinguishes a certain type of Calvinist theology, called covenantal or federal theology (in which since Adam God has related to people with a covenant of grace), from a Lutheran view (in which God related to people first under a covenant of law given by Moses and later under a covenant of grace), and later, from a dispensational view (in which God works with a number of different covenants at different times).

Also, *covenant* may refer to an understanding of the church as the voluntary gathering together of people of faith, in distinction from the understanding of the church as created by the gracious activity of God. Many Christians recognize the value of understanding the church both as a creation of God and as a fellowship of persons who covenant to worship and serve God together.

CREATION. The acts of God which brought the universe into existence and continue to sustain it. Christians have understood the account which is given in Genesis of the world's beginning to affirm that God created the world. He did not take something and make the world out of it, but rather caused all that is to be.

This is not the only understanding of God's relationship to the world. Pantheism equates God and the universe. Dualism, on the other hand, teaches that there are two eternal powers in the universe—good and evil—and that these two are constantly battling against one another. While maintaining that there is only one reality, such as the atom or mind, monism teaches that the universe is to be understood in nontheistic terms. Deism affirms that God created the world, but then withdrew from it and allows the universe to follow its own course.

Christian theology maintains that God is still involved in the world and especially with its inhabitants. The world is dependent on him for its existence. He caused it to be and through his power it continues to exist.

The world is finite, that is, it is limited. It has a beginning and will have an end. Only God is infinite. Since the nineteenth century, scientists have tried to explain the origin of the universe and particularly the origin of life on the earth. Many scientists accept evolution as a theory which best explains the diversity of living plants and animals. Evolution does not and cannot give an explanation for the origin of the universe, but only for some developments within it. The Christian doctrine of creation explains both the origin of the universe and the meaning of the developments within it. This has led many Christians to deny the theory of evolution but others to affirm that evolution is simply an explanation of how God does his work in the world.

There is no consensus on this subject among evangelical Christians today.

CREEDS. Official, summary statements of religious belief.

In the Old Testament, faith was confessed by reciting God's mighty acts of salvation, rather than making formal statements about God. Jews also recited daily Deuteronomy 6:4: "Hear, O Israel: The Lord our God is one Lord." Belief in one God rather than many was unique to Israel and central to Israel's faith.

In the New Testament, there are traces of early Christian creeds. Some are very short, such as "Jesus Christ is Lord" (Phil. 2:11 and elsewhere), and others more closely approximate the detailed statements of later centuries, such as 1 Timothy 3:16.

Some creeds grew out of confessions learned and recited by candidates for baptism; this is the origin of the Apostles' Creed. Other creeds were officially adopted by councils of church leaders, such as the Nicene Creed. Baptismal creeds usually begin with the words "I believe" and counciliar creeds with the words "We believe." The structure of the Apostles' and Nicene creeds, and of others in the early church, is tripartite. The first part is about God the Father, the second about God the Son, and the third about God the Holy Spirit.

In addition to the early creeds which are accepted by virtually all Christians, following the Reformation the various Protestant churches developed creeds which expressed their particular understanding of Christian faith. The Church of England has its Thirty-Nine Articles, the Presbyterians have their Westminster Confession, and the Lutherans have Martin Luther's Catechisms.

Some Protestants, including Baptists, have rejected creeds. They insist that the Bible alone is authoritative for Christian faith and practice and that Christians should not be coerced into accepting a human creed. Even so, they are willing to make confessions of faith, which are very similar in form and content to traditional creeds; for example, the Second London Confession of English Baptists was deliberately modeled on the Westmin-

---

ster Confession. The difference between a creed and a confession is in the authority attributed to them and in the use to which they are put.

D

DEACON. An ordained, lay servant of the church.

It is not certain that the seven chosen in Acts 6:1-6 to minister to Greek widows in the early church were the first deacons. But this group did provide a pattern for the modern diaconate, namely, that deacons are servants of the church.

In some denominations, for example among Roman Catholics, the office of deacon is a stage one goes through in preparation for ordination as a minister or priest. The role of deacon in Baptist churches has varied. In some settings, deacons have functioned as a board of directors making decisions on behalf of the local congregation. More recently the role of deacon has shifted back toward ministry. In this role, the deacon is a leader in helping members of the congregation as well as in the decision-making process within the local church. Deacons have traditionally had the responsibility of distributing the bread and cup at the Lord's Supper. The deacon has always been the pastor's chief helper (Phil. 1:1).

Qualifications for deacons are set forth in Acts 6:3 and 1 Timothy 3:8-13. Qualifications that have been most widely debated concern whether a deacon must be a man and whether a divorced person may serve as a deacon. The New Testament seems to be clear on the first issue. There were women deacons in the first century (Rom. 16:1). However, it is not certain whether the duties of the women deacons were different from those of their male counterparts. The divorce issue is less clear, though many scholars believe that Paul was concerned about polygamy rather than divorce in the diaconite (1 Tim 3:8-13).

Ordination has typically involved: being chosen by the church to serve; submitting to an ordination council composed of deacons and ministers; and an ordination service which includes the laying on of hands by the ordained deacons and ministers present as well as, in some cases, the congregation.

The word *deacon* means minister. Jesus said of himself, "I have come to minister" (see Mark 10:45). Thus, when the deacons serve the church, they are following the example of Jesus himself.

DEATH. The cessation of life.

The Christian understands death in two senses. First, it is a normal condition of the created world. All physical things change and decay; all living things die.

Second, death is associated with sin and guilt. Adam and Eve died because they disobeyed God, and Paul wrote that "the wages of sin is death" (Rom. 6:23). This Christian teaching is confirmed by the fear of death which is virtually universal among all people.

In the Old Testament, little was said about hope for life after death. In the New Testament, however, the resurrection of Jesus led the early church to affirm vigorously that the life which Christ provides cannot be lost, even in death. Concern about life after death is widespread in the world, even in scientifically-minded, developed countries in the late twentieth century.

Death should be distinguished from dying, which is the process leading up to death. In the case of sudden accidents, the process of dying is extremely brief, but many persons know for months or even years that they are involved in the process of dying. Ministry to these persons is very important, and the church is now giving attention to the special needs of the terminally ill.

The church has provided funeral services for the dead almost from the beginning, just as it provides special services for other important passages in life (birth, adolescence, and marriage). The purpose of funerals varies, but it may include celebration of the victory over death which Christ gives, remembering the deceased, and comforting the bereaved. The victory over death sometimes is misconstrued in funerals, as when it is said that death is a friend rather than an enemy, for example. Death is no friend of humanity. Christ is our friend, and he overcomes death on behalf of his people.

DENOMINATION. A church or sect within Christianity, especially in the United States.

The earliest Christian church was a single, united community of faith. Jesus prayed for the unity of his followers (John 17:11). Early Christians experienced divisions of various kinds (see, for example, 1 Cor. 1:12) and, as the church went out into the Roman Empire, spread out geographically. But there was a profound sense that all the followers of Jesus were members of a single body of Christ.

In the patristic era, the church lost members to various groups, such as Montanists, Arians, Donatists, and so on. But these groups never claimed simply to be alternate denominations; they claimed to be the true church, and their claims had to be evaluated on those terms.

The first great rift in the church was between the Eastern Orthodox and Roman Catholic Churches. Tensions began in the ninth century, and the separation was complete in the eleventh century. The issues contributing to the division were both theological and practical.

The second great division was the Protestant Reformation of the sixteenth century. It resulted in the formation out of Roman Catholicism of national churches, such as the Church of England, the Lutheran Church, and the Reformed Churches. Each of these churches was established as the state religion in one or more states, so that they were not denominations in the modern sense.

The Reformation also produced radical groups, some of whom had no political benefactors and wanted none. These groups, such as Anabaptists and Mennonites, learned to practice their faith in countries where there was an established church which allowed them some tolerance. However, they often were persecuted.

The United States was created without an established

religion (some of the constituent states had themselves had state religions, however), and its Bill of Rights promised freedom of religion to its citizens. From its earliest history, this country has had no state church but many religious bodies. These are denominations. As other nations have permitted more religious freedom, they too have come to perceive of the divisions of Christians as denominations.

Religious liberty requires that alternative forms of theology and church life and polity be permitted to exist. While the existence of denominations is regrettable—since Christ wants his people to be one (John 17:21)—it is not as regrettable as efforts to coerce people into belief. Denominationalism is the price we have paid for authentic religious liberty.

E

ECUMENISM. The movement to unite the church.

The ecumenical movement is a twentieth-century phenomenon. The church has been divided almost from its inception. At first there were Jews and Gentiles, then there were Roman Catholics and Eastern Orthodox, now there are hundreds of denominations, sects, and churches which call themselves Christians but have no real ties to one another. Many Christians have desired through the centuries to heal these divisions. The apostle Paul was perhaps the first and most successful ecumenist. He was able to get the Jewish Christians to accept the Gentile Christians as members of the church without their accepting the Jewish ceremonial legalism.

The word *ecumenism* comes from a Greek word meaning *the whole world*. Ecumenists have tried to unite the whole Christian world. To this end the modern ecumenical movement has taken two forms. The first form has been an attempt to reunite Christians into an organized union—to have one church. This has proven to be impossible, though there have been instances of union among various Christian denominations.

Southern Baptists have carefully avoided such unions on the grounds that theological purity would be compromised.

The other form of ecumenism has emphasized Christian cooperation. Baptists have done this willingly—on the mission field, on political issues, and at the local church level.

All Christians have the mandate from Jesus to strive for oneness within the arena of authentic religious liberty. The goal of that unity is for us to be united to one another as Christ is to the Father (John 17:21).

ESCHATOLOGY. The doctrine of last things.

All religions are not concerned about the future. The Jewish religion is very concerned with the future of the world. Through the prophets, a hope was planted in the hearts of the Jewish people.

The New Testament teaches that Jesus Christ both fulfilled the hopes of the Old Testament and raised new hopes in the hearts of his followers. Broadly speaking, the hope that he fulfilled was the hope for the coming of Messiah. "Jesus is the Christ" (see Mark 8:29) means that Jesus is the long-awaited person anointed and sent by God to act on God's behalf and to provide redemption for the oppressed people of God. The Christian preaching that Jesus rose from the dead meant that an old age was drawing to a close and a new era was dawning in the relations of God and people, for resurrection was definitely an eschatological or end-time event for Jews. Peter's sermon at Pentecost (Acts 2) shows how important the fulfillment of Old Testament hopes was to the faith of the early church.

The hope which Jesus raised for his followers differed from the Old Testament hope principally in that it included hope for life after death, as well as hope for the future life of people on the earth. How did the early church come to hope for life after death? Although it drew upon teachings about resurrection which had developed in Judaism after the close of the Old Testament, the real source of Christian hope is found in the resurrection of Jesus from the dead. Without that event there would have been no church, no Christian faith, and no Christian hope (see 1 Cor. 15:13-15). Because of that event, there was a new community of faith with a new experience of God's love. That community was convinced that nothing in this world or the next could ever separate them from the love God had given in Jesus Christ (see Rom. 8:28).

Eschatology thus comprises two subjects: in one, Jesus is the fulfillment of hope; and in the other, he is the source of new hope. The traditional ingredients in eschatology have been the doctrines of the *parousia* or coming of Christ (*second coming* is not a biblical term), the resurrection, the judgment, and heaven and hell. The source of belief in the *parousia* was Jesus Christ himself. He taught that his followers would one day see the Son of man coming on clouds of glory (for example, Matt. 25:31 *ff.*). The early church maintained a lively hope that Christ would come, perhaps in their own lifetime (see 1 Thess. 4:13-18; this letter probably is the earliest of the New Testament documents). That hope has endured, in one form or another, throughout the church's history.

ETERNAL LIFE. The never-ending experience of living with God.

In the Old Testament, the Jews did not believe in a meaningful afterlife. They understood life after death to be a shadowy existence of no real importance. Toward the end of the Old Testament period, some Jews began to teach and believe in resurrection and a meaningful life after death. When Jesus came on the scene, there was still a controversy brewing among Jews as to whether there would be a day of resurrection. The Sadducees did not believe it; the Pharisees did (Matt. 22:23).

In the New Testament, the meaning of eternal life is closely tied to faith in Christ. Not only do Christians have the promise of life after death (John 3:16) but we also have the assurance of the quality of that future life through our experiences with the Holy Spirit in the present (John 10:10). Eternal life, then, begins with a person's conversion experience and continues for eternity. Christians believe that this eternal life will grow to be increasingly meaningful and rich as one moves from this world into the next.

EVANGELICAL. A term based on the Greek word for gospel (*euangelion,* good news), therefore, referring to any person, church, or teaching which is true to the Christian gospel.

Throughout the history of the church certain groups have felt that the church at large had distorted or displaced the gospel. They have attempted to call the church back to the gospel, and for that reason they have sometimes taken the name *evangelical.* Thus the Protestant Reformers referred to their teachings and practices as evangelical in contrast to those of the Roman Church. The Wesleyan revival in the eighteenth century was called "the evangelical awakening" because it called the church away from formality and deadness into a warmhearted experience of the gospel. Theological conservatives in the twentieth century are called *evangelical* because they are attempting to call the church back to the traditional truths of the gospel. Other examples could be given.

In European Christianity, the word has a special usage. Neither Luther nor Calvin wanted a church to be named for him. Thus churches which follow Calvin's teachings are called *Reformed,* and those which follow Luther's teachings are called *Evangelical.*

The word *evangelical* is sometimes confused with the word *evangelistic.* Though their etymologies are identical, in modern English their meanings are distinct. To be evangelical is to be committed to the gospel of Jesus Christ; this commitment may express itself in theology, in worship, in service, and in other forms. To be evangelistic is to attempt actively to spread the gospel to those who are not Christians.

EVANGELISM. The act of sharing the gospel with the hope of making converts.

The word *evangelism* means *the preaching of the gospel.* There are varying evangelism strategies: mass evangelism which utilizes the media and large crusades; impersonal evangelism, such as preaching on the street corner; personal evangelism, such as door-to-door canvassing; and cultivative evangelism whereby one shares his faith with a person after befriending or ministering to him. All of these strategies are designed to carry out Christ's Great Commission (Matt. 28:19-20).

One of the recognized offices of the early church was that of the evangelist (Eph. 4:11). Many churches still recognize this office as a distinct calling.

For Christians, evangelism is not an option but a mandate. God is a sending God (John 3:16). Jesus sent his disciples to evangelize and proclaimed the kingdom himself through preaching and teaching, calling on all men to repent (Mark 6:7-13). The Holy Spirit equips the church to share the gospel and leads the world to receive it (John 20:21-23).

The message of Christian evangelism is the gospel, the claim that God was in Christ reconciling the world unto himself. The goal of Christian evangelism is to share that gospel with the entire world. The method of achieving that goal is for all Christians to be evangelistic.

EVIL. All the powers, events, persons, activities, relationships, and other realities which are contrary to the good purposes of God.

The Bible was written against the background of a limited dualism. Good and evil, light and darkness, are both real in the present world. However, only God is eternal, and God is good, so evil has not always existed, nor will it continue to exist following the consummation of God's purpose. In the meantime, however, evil is very real and pervasive in the world.

Two kinds of evil are distinguishable. One is moral evil, or sin, which is a deliberate act of disobedience toward God by a free person. The first sinners were Adam and Eve (see Gen. 3). All human beings who reach the age of accountability become sinners.

The second type of evil is natural evil, and it may be analyzed in various ways. It includes illness, suffering, death, ignorance, and perhaps ugliness. Its origin is nowhere discussed in the Bible. Clearly much natural evil is a result of moral evil; for example, much suffering is caused by sin. Some natural evil is not a result of moral evil, so far as can be observed. Some Christians believe as an article of faith that all natural evil is a result of human disobedience;

others believe, also as an article of faith, that some natural evil was created by God so that the world would be an appropriate environment for people to grow in love for God and for one another.

Both of these views have been developed as part of a theodicy, an effort to show that God's ways are always righteous in spite of the existence of evil, particularly, of relatively innocent, pointless human suffering. Suffering is the most serious difficulty faced by the Christian understanding of God as both all-loving and all-powerful.

Christianity has traditionally spoken of a being who is the embodiment of all evil, namely, the devil. The modern picture may owe more to John Milton than to the Bible. What the Bible presents is a creature, variously called the serpent, Satan, the devil (accuser), Lucifer, the enemy, the tempter, and the god of this world. His relation to demons, so clear in Milton, is not worked out in the Bible (see Matt. 25:41, Jude 6), nor is his origin discussed (though an ancient tradition associates the devil with the king of Babylon in Isa. 14:12-15). His activities include tempting human beings (Gen. 3), accusing God's people (Job 1—2), and in every way opposing God's purposes. The ministry of Jesus included a struggle against the devil (Matt. 4; Luke 11:20-22) and the exorcism or casting out of demons. The salvation which Christ provides includes deliverance from all evil forces (Eph. 2:1-10). The Christian hope is that in the future all evil shall be destroyed, including the devil (Rev. 20:7-10).

Belief in a literal devil, in contrast to the devil as a symbol for all evil, has been challenged as superstitious by the secular, scientifically minded, and even those Christians who hold to the traditional belief often do so in a formal rather than an internalized way, so that they do not normally live as if the devil or demons are responsible for what they are experiencing. One popular scientific explanation for demon possession is that it is a primitive description of psychosomatic illness.

On the other hand, much of the population of the present world does not think in this way at all. They live, as people did in the first century, in prescientific circumstances, and buffetings of Satan are all too real to them. They respond enthusiastically to the message that says that Jesus Christ not only will forgive their sins but also will deliver them from the forces of darkness which oppress them.

And would it not be wise for even the most scientific minds to be reminded that renaming demon possession, for example, as schizophrenia, however helpful it may or may not be for understanding, does not resolve the problem? Citizens of advanced nations suffer no less from fears, guilt, compulsions, delusions, than citizens of underdeveloped countries. Though modern medical treatment is very helpful and gratitude for it is very important, the large population in mental institutions is evidence that the problem still exists. Death, which the Bible describes as the devil's ultimate weapon (Heb. 2:14), is the most universal form of evil, and it has not been and will not be eliminated by science.

F

FAITH. Trust in God. Christian faith is trust in God as he revealed himself in Jesus Christ.

Trust in God comprises two factors. The first is intellectual: one believes that God exists and that Jesus is his Son and humanity's Savior. The other factor goes beyond the intellectual to embrace the whole person; one believes in the God who acted in Jesus Christ; one accepts this God as one's own God, Savior, Father, and Friend. Both factors must be present for faith to be complete. An intellectual factor alone is no more than accepting information.

In the Old Testament, Abraham is the great example of faith. He had to trust God almost, as it were, in a vacuum, with little or no support from his environment. His descendants found many challenges to their faith, but they always received support, especially for the intellectual factor, from the fact that they belonged to a community of faith.

In the New Testament, Jesus both called upon his followers

to believe in the Father (Mark 11:22) and accepted their faith in himself (Mark 9:14-29). (The noun *faith* and the verb *believe* are the same root word in Greek, though not in English.) Paul regarded faith in Jesus Christ as the fundamental response to be made by a person who hears the gospel. Christian faith may quite properly be said to be in the Father, in the gospel, in Jesus Christ, or even in the blood or the resurrection of Jesus Christ.

Faith is not a good work which earns God's approval; it is the response made to his initiative in Christ, the acceptance of the new relationship of forgiveness and love. Neither is faith a matter of being credulous or gullible; it is an honest response to the truth one has heard and sincerely recognized as truth. Nor is faith something which can be coerced; it is a freely given response of a whole person to Jesus Christ. Christian faith is made possible by the proclamation of the gospel, and no one who has not heard the gospel can have Christian faith. Christian faith is a profoundly personal experience, but it is not private. Personal faith is supported by the faith of the church and, in turn, supports the faith of others.

The most wonderful thing that can happen to any human being is for him to come to trust God. Jesus makes it possible for people today to be intellectually honest, to be real persons, and to come to trust in God.

THE FALL. Humanity's loss of innocence through disobedience to God.

The Bible does not use the term *fall*, but the term is widely used in the Christian church to characterize the meaning of the story told in Genesis 2—3. The story is that the first parents of humanity yielded to the temptations of the serpent in Eden and disobeyed God's command not to eat of the tree of the knowledge of good and evil. They thus became sinners, and all of their descendants have inherited a nature and a world which are fallen or sinful. The Old Testament does not allude to this story again, but Paul used it to present his understanding both of sin and of the redemption provided by Christ (Rom. 5:12-21).

Three questions are asked concerning the fall. First, is the story in Genesis historical or mythological? To put it another way, does it tell of the fall of the parents of the human race, or does it rather tell a parable of the fall of every person? The answer is that while it may in a sense tell of the fall of every person, its primary message concerns the first parents. There are two reasons for saying this. First, the author of Genesis was clearly very concerned about beginnings (the word *genesis* means beginning), and in this story he told of the beginning of the human problem. Also, the story is that Adam and Eve might have gone either way: they were, so to speak, in a neutral environment. That aspect of the Genesis story does not apply to any person today. The world today is fallen; it is assuredly not the Garden of Eden.

With the above reservation, however, it is possible to accept the story as also a parable of the sin of every person, in much the same way that the story of the sin of David, for example, might serve as a parable for every person. Though it is not possible to know for certain that the author of Genesis intended this meaning, the name of the first man does suggest it; *Adam* means *man*.

The second question concerning the fall is, did it happen? Is there such a thing as freedom? Have human beings chosen to disobey God? The traditional Christian answer to these questions is yes, though there are those who doubt it. It has been said that the teaching about the fall is the most empirically verifiable of all major Christian doctrines.

Finally, what exactly are the results of the fall? Genesis hints at some: the couple was cast out of the Garden (out of the presence of God); they would suffer for their sins, the woman in childbearing and the man in hard labor; they were alienated from each other.

FELLOWSHIP. Shared life.

Throughout the Bible, God is pictured as working to create a community. In Genesis the Lord says: "It is not good that the man should be alone" (2:18). God created the nation Israel to be a people, his people. Old Testament writers acknowledged the importance of people living together in friendship: "Behold, . . . how pleasant it is for brethren to dwell together in unity" (Ps. 133:1, KJV).

The New Testament speaks of a fellowship which not only goes beyond the nationalism of Israel in the Old Testament but also is more intense and more spiritual, a "fellowship of the Holy Spirit" (2 Cor. 13:14). Jesus founded this new fellowship during his historical ministry and enlarged and enriched it by the gift of the Spirit. It is, therefore, a creation of God not of humanity, into which all people are called and in which they may share. This common life has the gospel at its center and love as its life-style. It has received gifts from God so that it may be able to build itself up in love.

Fellowship has been a part of the divine purpose throughout creation and redemption. It is, therefore, an end in itself. While fellowship is a resource for individual living and for the church's ministry, it is a mistake to regard fellowship as only a means to these or any other ends.

The Greek word for fellowship used in the New Testament (*koinonia*) may also be used of sharing money (2 Cor. 9:13) and of the Lord's Supper ("communion," 1 Cor. 10:16), both of which are understandable in view of the meaning of fellowship as sharing a life together.

FORGIVENESS. Pardon for sin.

Inasmuch as the experience of two persons becoming alienated because one has wronged the other is a universal human experience, most people recognize the need for forgiveness if personal relations are to be maintained. Alienation and reconciliation are, therefore, two of the most important themes in world literature.

In the Old Testament, these two themes surface as characterizing the relations of God and people. People are alienated from God because they have disobeyed his laws and broken their covenant relation with him. They deserve his punishment. Yet God is willing to forgive, that is, to forego punishment and to receive repentant sinners back into fellowship. The most famous individual example of this is David, who sinned flagrantly, repented heartily, and was forgiven freely (2 Sam. 11:2 to 12:25). There is a tradition which says that Psalm 51 is David's prayer of repentance and that Psalm 32 is his expression of gratitude when God forgave him.

The Old Testament also speaks of national sin, national repentance, and of God's forgiving the entire nation (as, Ps. 130). The message of some Old Testament prophets and of John the Baptist was a call to national repentance. Alongside the prophets who usually spoke as if God would forgive the repentant, Israel's priests maintained a system of sacrifices for the forgiveness of sins.

Jesus offended some of his hearers by claiming the authority to forgive sins, which was believed to be the prerogative of God alone (Mark 2:1-13). In the Lord's Prayer, he taught his followers to pray for divine forgiveness. At the Lord's Supper, he remarked that his blood would be shed on the cross for the forgiveness of sins (Matt. 26:28), an allusion to the Old Testament sacrifices; later Paul and other Christians, sometimes at length, developed the sacrificial idea that Christ had provided forgiveness through his blood (for example, Heb. 9:1 to 10:25). Jesus even prayed that the Father would forgive his executioners (Luke 23:34).

Early Christian preaching promised forgiveness to all who would repent and believe in Christ (Acts 2:38). So the church was from the beginning a community of forgiven sinners. Since they themselves had been forgiven, Christians were urged to exercise forgiveness toward all others (Eph. 4:32; Col. 3:13).

In the past, some Christians have believed that forgiveness is easy and cheap. This notion is present when forgiveness is treated merely as an overlooking of sin or a forgetting. More recently, the church has realized that forgiveness is actually a very costly experience; the more seriously one takes sin and the more fully one loves the sinner the more costly forgiveness becomes. This modern observation seems to capture a truth already present in the biblical language of the necessity of sacrifice for the forgiveness of sins.

Forgiveness is both negative and positive. Negatively, it is the withholding of punishment. Positively, it is free, full, unrestricted reconciliation. The loss of either of these aspects results in an impoverished understanding of divine forgiveness.

FREEDOM. The God-given capacity to make choices.

Freedom is one of God's greatest gifts to humanity. It allows us the dignity of making choices for ourselves. God does not abuse our freedom by forcing himself upon us, but we abuse it by rejecting his love and his desire to have a relationship with us.

Freedom may be taken from a person through torture or coercion, but when that is done the person is no longer fully human. His actions thus become morally void, for he has not freely chosen them. For example, a prisoner of war who is forced to reveal classified information through brainwashing, drugs, or torture should not be condemned as a betrayer of his fellow soldiers.

In one sense human beings are not free, for we are enslaved by sin. The corporate evil in our world prevents us from having the choices available to us which would allow us to be truly free. Often we must choose the lesser of two bad options because no good choice is available to us. Further, our own personal sins hamper our ability to choose the good.

The Christian gospel proclaims that a person may be freed from the restrictions of sin through faith in Christ (John 8:31). The Holy Spirit then comes into a person's life and begins to transform that person into the likeness of God. The Christian's freedom is still impaired, but he is freer than he could be otherwise. The freedom which is offered in the Christian life is not the freedom to abuse one's privileged relationship with God, but rather it is the freedom to be fully human (Rom. 6:1-2). Paradoxically, the more one submits to the Spirit's leadership, the freer he becomes. We see this freedom exemplified in the life of Jesus who came to freely "give his life as a ransom for many" (Mark 10:45).

The story of humanity's fall in the Garden of Eden is the story of impaired freedom. The story of Christ's death and resurrection is the story of how human freedom may be regained (Gal. 5:1).

G

GOD. The ultimate being, who is the Creator of the world.

The most distinctive teaching about God in the Old Testament was monotheism, the conviction that there are not many gods, but one and only one true and living God. For monotheists *God* is a name, whereas for polytheists *god* is a common noun. The Jewish people arrived at their conviction about monotheism by leaving behind polytheism (Abraham would have known polytheism in Ur, and the people of Israel would have experienced it in Egypt and again in Canaan) and, perhaps, henotheism (there are many gods, but the Lord is superior). From the point of view of Israel, the gods of their neighbors were frauds, not gods at all, but idols, and were to be destroyed (see Ps. 115).

In addition to moving from polytheism to monotheism, Old Testament understandings of God made three other moves. One was from nationalism to universalism. That is, Israel held a deep conviction that she had a unique covenant relation with God, a covenant summarized in the words, "I will be your God, and you will be my people." Thus, God was the God of Israel. But if there were only one true God, then God must also be the God of all the earth and of all the people of the earth. The prophets taught that God was Lord of other nations (for example, Amos 1). The Book of Jonah tells of God urging the prophet to take his message to Nineveh in Assyria. The conviction that God was the Creator of all the heavens and the earth meant that his interests and influence were not restricted in any way, not even to his beloved covenant people.

Another movement in Israel's understanding of God was from nature religion to history religion. In nature religion, gods are active and revealed primarily in the recurring cycles of nature, in birth and life and death, in seedtime, harvest, and winter. While Israel celebrated events, such as harvest, her emphasis was upon God's mighty acts in history. God had chosen and called Israel to be his people, delivered them from Egypt, given them the commandments for their national life, and given them a land flowing with milk and honey. The central religious observance in Israel's life was Passover, the remembering of God's mighty act of salvation at the Exodus. Theology was recital of God's acts, and worship was adoration of the God who had acted (see Ps. 105, for example).

A final movement in Israel's understanding of God was from ritualism to the priority of the moral. The Torah, which provided the structure for Israel's national life, did not separate government from religion or ritual from moral demand. Through the great prophets of the eighth and seventh centuries, Israel learned that in God's purposes for people, morality has priority over religious rituals, however valuable the latter may be. The Lord says: "I hate, I despise your feasts, and I take no delight in your solemn assemblies. But let justice roll down like waters, and righteousness like an ever-flowing stream" (Amos 5:21,24).

These movements occurred over centuries, and the lessons had to be relearned when they were forgotten. Together they give a picture of one true God, the God of all the earth, the God who acts in history to redeem, the God whose primary concerns are moral rather than ritual.

But this does not exhaust the Old Testament teaching about God. God both transcends the world and is closely related to it. That is, God is both the Holy One, utterly beyond the world, and the God who loves and cares intensely for his world, who pities those who fear him as a father pities his children (Ps. 103:13).

God is the Creator. This means the world is not eternal but depends upon the creative act of God for its existence. The world is not to be confused with God, but neither is the world a creation of the powers of darkness.

God reveals his name to his people. The most dramatic example of this is the revelation to Moses at the burning bush (Ex. 3:1-22, especially v. 14). His name is JHWH; he also is Adonai, the Lord; he is known to his people by the many names he has graciously revealed to them.

God is also known by adjectives. He is the loving, righteous, wise, powerful God. These and other perfectives are called in later theology the divine attributes.

While to the outside world, the outstanding Jewish contribution to civilization has been monotheism, in actual fact the Old Testament teaching about God is very complex and profound and far richer than the term *monotheism* suggests. As important for the development of Western civilization as the ideas of monotheism and creation have been, it is to be regretted that other equally important Old Testament understandings of God have not prevailed throughout Western culture.

But the Old Testament understanding of God does not exhaust the divine self-revelation given in the Bible. "In many and various ways God spoke of old to our fathers by the prophets," recorded the writer of Hebrews, and he added, "but in these last days he has spoken to us by a Son" (Heb. 1:1-2). The New Testament may be read as a record of the impact which Jesus Christ made upon the Jewish understanding of God.

So tremendous was the difference made by Jesus that it comes as a surprise to realize that he never directly challenged the Old Testament understanding of God. His impact was made indirectly. He did explicitly correct erroneous views held by his contemporaries. For example, some Jews assumed that God loved and accepted only those persons who kept the law. By his words and actions, Jesus showed that God loves and accepts even those who fall far short of the demands of the Torah, provided they accept his love (see Luke 15).

But concerning the Old Testament teaching itself, Jesus enriched rather than challenged it. He clarified its true meaning. For example, in response to a question—an insincere one, in fact—about the Torah, Jesus made clear that in God's sight love has priority over all the other commands, and, in fact, that love is the fulfillment of all that was required by the law and the prophets (Matt. 22:34-40).

Also, Jesus added to the teaching about God. The Old Testament had taught that God is a King who rules over the destinies of nations and the lives of people. To this teaching Jesus added a new revelation, namely, that in Jesus' own time, the kingdom of God was being extended into people's lives in a new and very important sense. The kingdom of God was at the center of Jesus' preaching.

Further, Jesus revealed that the coming of the kingdom was occurring precisely in his own life and work. Thus his work should be recognized as divine activity in the world. "If I by the power of God cast out demons, then the kingdom of God has come upon you" (see Luke 11:20). To recognize Jesus is to know God, and to reject Jesus is to not know God. "All things have been delivered to me by my Father; and no one knows who the Son is except the Father, or who the Father is except the Son and any one to whom the Son chooses to reveal him" (Luke 10:22).

The term *Father* is Jesus' most striking designation for God. He addressed God as "Abba," a very intimate term without precedent in earlier Jewish prayers. He knew himself to have a unique and close relationship with God. And he introduced his disciples into the same, new, wonderful, close relationship with God, for he instructed them, "Pray then like this: 'Our Father'" (Matt. 6:9). The fact that *Father* is now widely used in the Western world as a way of speaking of God should not blind us to the originality of the idea in Jesus' teachings.

In the Old Testament, God sometimes acted by sending his Spirit into the world (as, 1 Sam. 11:6). When Jesus began his public ministry the Spirit came upon him in a special way, equipping him to carry out his ministry in the power and with the guidance of the Spirit (Luke 3:21-22; 4:14,18). Jesus promised his followers that they too would receive the Spirit (Luke 12:9-13), a promise fulfilled on Pentecost (Acts 2).

Thus by life and teaching, Jesus enriched the Old Testament understanding of God. But there is more to be said. The question yet to be answered is, Who is Jesus? He himself forced his disciples to face the question, and he accepted Peter's word, "You are the Christ" (Mark 8:27-30). But that did not exhaust his meaning. Perhaps no one, at least no Jewish monotheist, could possibly grasp the ultimate truth about Jesus before his resurrection. After that event, the church was gradually led to see that, in fact, Jesus of Nazareth was none other than the unique Son of God, one with the Father, the very Word of God made flesh (John 1:1-14; 10:30).

The incarnation means two things for the understanding of God. First, God is more complex than the Jews had realized. Second, every event in Jesus' life was somehow also an event in the life of God. The former point meant that the church had to develop an understanding of God which, while true to monotheism, also went beyond it; this is called the doctrine of the Trinity. The latter point meant that the church had to learn to think of God not only as powerful but also as accepting weakness; not only as spiritual but also as living in the flesh; not only as bliss but also as suffering; not only as life but also as dying; not only as absolute but also as humble; not only as Lord but also as servant. Both of these tremendous implications began to be worked out in the New Testament; most Christians would agree that the church has yet to assimilate them fully into its understanding of God.

This, then, is a partial listing of the biblical teaching about God: God is one; Creator; transcendent and personal; God of all the earth; who commands moral behavior more than ritual and love over all else; who graciously revealed his names; who acts in history to save; who loves all people, good and bad; who extended his reign over people's lives through the work of Jesus; who is the Father of Jesus; and also who was incarnate as Jesus; whose Spirit guided and empowered Jesus, and guided and empowered the followers of Christ; who is Father, and Son, and Holy Spirit. Since much of this is familiar to most Christians, it is well to remind ourselves that none of this—not one item in it— should ever be taken for granted. It is all given by revelation and is overwhelming in its importance. No one has ever understood fully all that this means. Since God is the God of the future, and since the Spirit guides Christians into all truth, it may be hoped that throughout life each Christian may come to deeper and truer appreciation for what God is like.

Is this only a reverent sentiment, or is fuller understanding actually possible? It is possible. Four examples may be given. First, the summary includes many statements about God's character and activities. But it includes no statement about his purpose in continual redemption. This is because the divine purpose has rarely been spoken of in the church. Some feel that reverence requires that nothing be said, that all be left as mystery. Surely mystery will remain, yet may nothing be said? Did not Paul attempt to state the purpose of God in his Letter to the Ephesians? Does not the Bible authorize us to say something, however inadequate?

It is not enough to say, God's purpose is to save sinners, for one wants to ask, What for? Nor is it enough to say, God's purpose is to bring glory to himself, for that fails to take serious account of his unselfish, gracious love. Both these things are true, but more is needed. The suggestion offered here is that God's purpose is to create a community of persons who freely accept God as their God and receive his love into their lives (through faith in Jesus Christ), and who respond to God by loving him with all their hearts, (that is, glorifying God), and by loving their neighbors as themselves, and who thereby bring glory to God. This is offered as a suggestion for further thinking.

To achieve a fuller understanding of God, three other questions must be answered.

First, is the God of the Bible the same as the God known to philosophers and to pagans? In other words, does God prepare the hearts of non-Christians to receive the gospel by giving them glimpses of himself? When philosophers speak of the One or the Ultimate or the Real or Being, do they witness to a truth, however partial, about God? Or should this idea be dismissed, as the Jews dismissed the gods of their neighbors as idols?

Second, and closely related to the above, can God's existence be proved? When the Bible was written, there were no atheists or virtually none. All were religious. Their only question was, Which God (gods)? The twentieth century is different. Many people today are secular. They are not convinced that there really is a God. What should a Christian do? Should he attempt to defend his belief, argue for it, give reasons for it? Or should he offer no help to unbelief?

Finally, how can God be both one and three? How can we understand God both as the Shema presents him—"Hear, O Israel, the Lord our God is one Lord" (Deut. 6:4)—and also take seriously the fact that Jesus is the Savior, the Lord, and, yes, the God, of Christians? Perhaps more than any other Christian conviction, this one cries out to be understood in a more profound and more Christian way.

GOSPEL. The good news about Jesus Christ.

Jesus proclaimed the gospel of God and his kingdom, which means that he preached the good news that through his life and work God was acting to extend his sovereign rule over the lives of people in a new way (Mark 1:14-15; see also Eph. 1:17-18). When the early church began to proclaim the gospel, it centered its message upon the events of Good Friday and Easter. In the death and resurrection of Jesus, God had acted decisively to provide salvation from sin (Acts 2:14-39; 1 Cor. 15:1-7).

Three questions are asked concerning the gospel. First, what is its historical extent? Does it include only the death and resurrection of Christ, or does it also include his life and work? There is no need to be too precise here. Jesus' death is continuous with his life. The entire Christ event is God's act, and is good news. The cross gathered up into one moment the entire meaning of his life. The gospel is Christ, especially his sacrifice.

Second, does the gospel include human response? Is it part of the good news that those who repent will be forgiven? The answer to this is that the gospel is the good news of God's work, whereas repentance is our response to the work of God. The gospel is good news, in fact, whether or not we respond to it; though, of course, one must respond in order to benefit fully from God's act.

Finally, is the gospel the experience of Christian living? Those who respond to the good news of God's great saving act begin a pilgrimage in which they experience God's grace in many ways: in the community of faith, in a new purpose for living, in hope for the future, in comfort for distress, in gifts for service, and so on. These good gifts and others are not themselves the gospel but are benefits which flow out of God's great, decisive act in the history of Jesus Christ.

No reduction of the Christian message to the ideals of Jesus or to the faith of people or to the benefits Christ gives is true to the gospel of the New Testament. The central fundamental Christian message remains what it always has been: Christ died for our sins according to the Scriptures, he was buried, and on the third day he rose from the dead (1 Cor. 15:1-7).

GRACE. The love of God which prompts him to save sinners.

In the Old Testament, God is pictured as being gracious—just yet loving (Ex. 34:6-7). Noah is said to have found grace, or acceptance, from God (Gen. 6:8).

It was the grace, or unfailing love, of God which caused him to lead the Israelites out of captivity and into the Promised Land (Ex. 15:13).

In the Old Testament, God's love for humanity is tied to the law. God's covenant promised that those who obeyed his law would receive his grace. Because people failed to obey the law, God through Christ established a new covenant. Unlike the old covenant, this new agreement does not depend on human ability. Instead God acted to meet humanity's deepest need; he sent his Son into the world to die for human sin. Our side of the agreement is to trust Jesus—to believe that he is God's solution for our sin problem. Thus, under the new covenant, we cannot earn our salvation or forgiveness, but rather we receive it as a gift (Rom. 3:21-24).

God's graciousness does not end with the conversion experience. His unfailing love continues to support and encourage Christians as they mature in the faith. This process of change and maturation which God works in our lives is called sanctification.

God's grace will continue to operate in our lives until we become like him (1 Thess. 5:23 *f.*).

HEAVEN. The home of God and the final destiny of the people of God.

In the Old Testament, heaven was understood to be above the sky. It was a spatial term. Jewish hopes for the future were centered on the present world rather than on heaven after death.

In the New Testament, heaven is still the home of God, as seen in the Lord's Prayer: "Our Father who art in heaven" (Matt. 6:9). The spatial idea remains: the Holy Spirit descended from heaven (Matt. 3:16), and Jesus ascended to heaven (Acts 1:9-11).

To this the New Testament adds the idea that heaven is the final home of all God's people. While it is not explicitly stated that Christians "go to heaven," the idea is presented symbolically: People of faith long for "a better country, that is, a heavenly one" (Heb. 11:16). God has prepared a new heaven and a new earth, a city radiant with the light of God's own glory (Rev. 21), to be the home of his people.

For many centuries the Bible's symbolic language about heaven was a source of joy and a subject for imaginative reflection, as the art of medieval churches attests. In the more secular age of the twentieth century, this language has become suspect and is an offense to many people, even to some Christians, who may be heard to say that they don't want to "stand on golden streets strumming a harp for eternity." What is needed today is a recovery of appreciation for biblical language in which heaven is presented, for therein lies a message of hope which can bring joy to people today, a hope that human beings may find their true identities in an eternal community of love and trust which worships God and is never threatened by evil or interrupted by death.

HELL. The eternal destiny of those who are not saved.

The Bible contains three words for *hell*. In the Old Testament, the Hebrew word *Sheol* represented the home of the dead (Gen. 37:35). It is described as a place of darkness (Job 17:13) and a place from which there is no return (Job 7:9).

In the New Testament, two words are used for *hell*. One word is *Hades*. *Hades*, like *Sheol*, is the place of the dead (Acts 2:27-31). Christ has power over *Hades* (Rev. 1:18).

The other word is *Gehenna*. *Gehenna* was a valley outside Jerusalem where garbage was dumped. The Jews believed that it was the place where the final judgment would take place. It is used to describe the place of punishment after death for the ungodly (Mark 9:43). *Gehenna* was associated with divine punishment, while *Hades* and *Sheol* were not.

Concerning eternal punishment, Christians have advanced a number of interpretations: eternal punishment of the wicked, annihilation of the wicked, or salvation of the wicked through some special work of God. Some Christians see weaknesses in all these views. For example, if God eternally punishes or annihilates the wicked, then in what sense does he win a complete, final victory? If he redeems them after death, then in what sense has he respected the decision which many people make to reject him? Christians can take consolation in the fact that it is God who is the Judge. His judgment will be in keeping with his character, and he is righteous and just.

The Christian gospel is not about eternal punishment but about eternal salvation. It is significant that the earliest Christian preaching, as recorded in Acts, did not contain a message about eternal punishment. That all people shall be judged by God is the clear teaching of Scripture. Jesus Christ is the norm by which we shall be judged.

HERESY. Unorthodox, nontraditional theology.

The Greek word *hairesis* literally means a choice. It occurs several times in the New Testament, but in only one passage is it used to mean unorthodox doctrine (2 Pet. 2:1).

The church has always attempted to state in general terms

what the meaning of God's revelation is, and persons who have deliberately rejected this have been resisted as heretics by the church. Thus Paul resisted Judaizers who felt that obedience to all the law was necessary for a person to be accepted by God (Gal. 1:6-9; 3:1-5), and John resisted Docetists who said that Jesus did not really have a human body (1 John 4:1-3). The practice of identifying untrue teachings and isolating unacceptable teachers was continued after the close of the New Testament.

Many people today find heresy hunting repugnant, but it is the unkind and unfair treatment of heretics which is so offensive. On the other hand, it is difficult to see how the church could have maintained its message over the centuries without identifying falsifications of it.

In God's providence, heretics have unwittingly been a help to the church, for they have forced the church to articulate more fully its convictions. An outstanding example of this is the fourth-century priest Arius, whose denial of the full deity of Jesus led the church to the thorough and balanced affirmations about Jesus which are embodied in the Nicene Creed.

HISTORY. Events which occurred in the past; also, the story of those events.

History as both events and story played an enormous role in biblical religion. The Jews believed that God had acted in history to redeem his people. They told that story as part of their heritage and celebrated those events as part of their worship (see, for example, Deut. 4).

Christians naturally followed the Jews in this, and they proclaimed as good news the story of God's great redeeming act in Jesus Christ and particularly his death and resurrection (1 Cor. 15:1-7). The history they interpreted and presented was not merely an illustration for the substance of their message; it was the substance.

For most of the church's history, the historical character of this proclamation posed no special intellectual problem, but the development of modern historical studies created a problem. Critical history is not an unquestioning recounting of past events, a mere compilation of chronicles. It is a deliberate putting of questions to the historical documents and other data used in reconstructing the past, together with a conscious effort to decide what really happened. Historians who have learned to interrogate their sources in this manner feel a moral obligation to do so, since the procedure is an honest quest to learn the truth about the past. They also feel a deep conviction that all conclusions about the past are tentative; historical knowledge can be more or less probable but never absolutely certain.

When the New Testament—the only important source for learning about the events of Jesus' life and work—was examined in this way, a new problem emerged for Christian faith. Could a historical judgment, which could never be more than probable, be indispensable for Christian faith? Christians became divided on the subject. Some felt that historical conclusions were not vital to faith, since faith is awakened in the heart by the proclamation of Christ, not arrived at by a critical study of the documents of the New Testament. Others believed that apart from an acceptance of the New Testament story of Jesus Christ as historically true, faith in God could not be fully Christian.

Several arguments are offered in support of the latter, more traditional view. One is that the church ought to go on proclaiming the history of Jesus Christ since it has always done so, as indeed it has. A second is that the history provided evidence in support of faith. A third is that great theological affirmations, such as "God is love," have their meaning precisely in the story of Jesus ("God is love" means Christ died for our sins and arose) and are evacuated of meaning if the history is forfeited.

It is difficult to see how this third argument can be refuted. This means, then, that if a person's personal trust in God is in fact distinctly Christian faith, it includes a conviction that certain events in the history of Jesus, notably his resurrection, really happened. One question to be dealt with by those who hold that history is in fact indispensable to Christian faith and who also accept the moral obligation to attempt to use the sources in order to determine what actually happened in the past, is, Which history? Which events are indispensable, and which are not? The question of the relation of history to faith remains one of the major concerns of contemporary theology.

HOLY SPIRIT. The Spirit of God and of Jesus Christ, the third person of the Trinity, who now guides the church and all Christians in their world mission.

In the Old Testament, references to the Spirit of the Lord occur frequently. The Spirit came to individual leaders, such as Bezaleel, Gideon, Samson, Saul, David, Micah, and Ezekiel. The Spirit gave them spiritual gifts, such as the skills of a craftsman, ability to judge, military skills, physical strength, authority to rule, prophecy, and visions (for example, Ex. 31:3; Judg. 6:34; 14:6; 1 Sam. 10:1-7; 2 Sam. 13:1-2; Mic. 3:8; Ezek. 8:3). These gifts were for special missions, and the Spirit is nowhere said to be present with all God's people. Nor did he stay permanently, for he left Saul and went to be with David, who feared that he too might lose the Spirit by sinning (1 Sam. 11:6; Ps. 51:10-11). The Old Testament also contains prophecies about a future time at which God's Spirit would be given to all God's people, to ordinary people as well as great leaders (Joel 2:28-32).

Jesus' entire life was associated with the Spirit, from his birth (Matt. 1:18), the beginning of his public ministry (Matt. 4:1-11), his temptation (Mark 1:12), through his entire public ministry (Luke 4:14). He was permanently guided and empowered by the Spirit. He was thus a unique bearer of the Spirit, and he promised that his followers could also receive the Spirit in the future (Luke 11:13; Mark 13:11; Acts 1:4-5).

John's Gospel records five times when Jesus spoke of the Spirit as the *Paraclete*, which means helper or comforter (John 14:16,26; 15:26; 16:7,13). He clearly distinguished the Spirit from himself by saying that only after he had departed from the earth would the Spirit come (John 16:7). But he also emphasized that the Spirit's work is clearly related to Jesus, for he will glorify Christ (John 16:14), bear witness concerning Christ (John 15:26), and remind the disciples of Christ (John 14:26).

Both the prophecies of the Old Testament concerning the

Spirit and the promises of Jesus concerning the Spirit were fulfilled on the Day of Pentecost (Acts 2:1-42). The Spirit was given to every Christian there (v. 3). This is the most complete revelation of the Spirit in the Bible and indicates clearly that the Spirit is divine and personal. The Spirit enabled Peter and the other disciples to proclaim the good news about Jesus Christ, and he thus initiated the Christian world mission. This is a clear fulfillment of the saying of Jesus in John that when the Spirit comes he will bear witness concerning Christ.

Paul experienced the Spirit just as the other early Christians did. In the churches, he saw a continuation of what had begun at Pentecost: the church continued to carry out its mission, guided, empowered, and equipped by the Spirit. The Spirit equipped the church for its work by giving gifts to believers (1 Cor. 12:1 to 13:13) and by giving gifted leaders to the churches (Eph. 4:7-16). He also worked to transform Christians into better persons by producing the moral fruits, of which the most important by far is love (Gal. 5:22). Paul followed the earlier Christians also in closely identifying the Spirit with Christ, even referring to him as the Spirit of Christ (Rom. 8:9; Gal. 4:6).

Since the close of the New Testament, the church has not often had to speak officially concerning the Spirit. At the Council of Constantinople (AD 381), the bishops declared that the Spirit was divine and to be "worshipped together and glorified together" with the Father and the Son. The church has had to try to balance the need for stability and order within the church with the possibility of the Spirit's working outside the orderly structures. There is a temptation for the church to try to capture the Spirit in its structures and also a temptation for individuals to resist the institutional church in the name of the Spirit. The same issue turns up in terms of revelation: the church usually says that God's revelation in the Bible is sufficient while some individuals claim that the Spirit is giving them new revelations.

In the twentieth century, the Pentecostal movement, and later the charismatic movement, insisted for the first time in history that all Christians should have a second experience with the Holy Spirit (after conversion) and that the sign that they had

had that experience was that they would speak in tongues. This movement is now firmly established both in Pentecostal denominations and within the churches of virtually all Protestant denominations and in Roman Catholicism. It raises the question whether a person actually has received the Spirit unless he speaks in tongues. The church at large has responded that all in whose hearts Christ dwells have received the Spirit (see Rom. 8:9) and that the test of the Spirit's presence is not tongues but fidelity to the gospel and love for the Christian community (see 1 Cor. 12:1 to 13:13). Some churches are tolerant toward the charismatic experience, while others oppose it vigorously.

A traditional way for the church to speak of God the Father is to describe his attributes (love, holiness, wisdom, power, and so on). A traditional way to speak of the Son is to enumerate events in his life (born in Bethlehem, grew up in Nazareth, baptized in the Jordan, ministered in Galilee, crucified in Jerusalem, raised the third day). The traditional way to speak of the Spirit is to list his activities (inspired the writers of the Bible, regenerates believers, gives gifts, guides and empowers the church). This procedure is a very satisfactory one. When it is followed, special emphasis should be given to the relation of the Spirit, in all his activities, to Christ: he draws people to Christ, he makes the gospel of Christ to become a living reality in people's lives, he reminds the church of Jesus Christ. This emphasis is needed to help the church to remember that the Spirit is not just any Spirit and not primarily linked with success, or enthusiasm, or wisdom, but with the gospel of Jesus Christ.

HOPE. The Christian confidence that the future is in the hands of God.

Christians have hope for themselves and for others because of what Jesus Christ accomplished in his life, through his death, and by his resurrection. This hope is normally thought of as hope for life after death and is assured to us by the presence of Christ in our lives.

The Christian hope is not merely for immortality of the soul but also for resurrection of the body. Though we shall be the same persons after death, there will be changes. The goal of life eternal is not to remain what we are but to become more like God. When Christians affirm the resurrection of the body, they are saying that there will be a continuity between our earthly bodies and our spiritual bodies (1 Cor. 15:44). Likewise our hope for resurrection does not rest upon the natural immortality of the soul but on our relationship to Christ. Eternal life is a gift from God (John 3:16).

The Christian hope may be contrasted with other views of life after death. Hindu theology, for instance, teaches that people undergo series of rebirths until finally perfected and made holy. Christians, on the other hand, maintain there is only one rebirth and that is into the life of Christ.

Christians have hope not only for life after death but also for the future of life on earth. The Christian believes that individuals and even societies can be radically transformed through the presentation and acceptance of the gospel. The Christian has hope not in himself or herself but in the God who loves the world enough to send his Son to save it (John 3:16). Without such confidence, Christians are of all people most to be pitied (1 Cor. 15:19).

IDOLATRY. Treating anything other than God as if it were God.

So long as religions held that there are many gods, the concept of idolatry did not occur. One worshiped one's own god or gods, and other people worshiped their gods. Beginning with Abraham, the Lord taught his people that he alone was the true and living God.

What, then, was the truth about the gods of other people? They were idols made by human hands, unable to speak or act, and to worship them was a self-destructive activity (Ps. 115). They had a reality, but not the reality claimed for them.

Followers of the true God, the Creator, must renounce all idols and have no dealings with them. Israel struggled for centuries to break away from the influence of these other gods.

Christianity, like Judaism, was born in a world in which other gods, or idols, were worshiped. Early Christians were often Gentiles who "turned to God from idols, to serve a true and living God" (1 Thess. 1:9). No effort was made to deny the reality of idols, and idolatry was understood as being at the root of the sinfulness of Gentiles (Rom. 1:18-23).

The success of Christianity in the Western world has meant the elimination of idols, that is, of metal or stone figures who are worshiped as gods. Unfortunately, another kind of idolatry has replaced the old, for people are always tempted to trust as the ultimate reality something which is less than the true God. Leading idols of our time have included political organizations and programs, economic systems, education, psychological therapies, money, family, fame, and power. Although one may not consciously worship these, one may care more about them than about God. One of the problems with idolatry of this kind is that it is so subtle as to be almost unrecognizable. For example, a business person may be ultimately concerned about financial success. Financial success is a good thing, but to have it as one's ultimate concern is idolatry. In perhaps the most ironic twist of all, one can even make an idol of aspects of the Christian faith: to revere the Bible, a church, a theological system, or a minister more than God is idolatry.

The only solution to idolatry is to remind oneself repeatedly that the Lord alone is God, and we should put no other gods before him.

IMAGE OF GOD. The likeness of man to God.

The phrase *image of God* appears in two Old Testament passages (Gen. 1:26-27; 9:6). One of these instances refers to the creation story in which God said, "Let us make man in our image." Some scholars believe the similarity spoken of was physical, while others think it refers to spiritual qualities. Though there have been a number of opinions offered as to the meaning of the phrase, no consensus has emerged. The reason for this is simple: the Bible nowhere states exactly what the image is. Since the image of God is what is unique to humans, it may be equated with personhood. In modern English usage, the word *personal* is what sets human beings apart from the other creations of God.

In the New Testament, the word is applied to Jesus. He is the image of God (2 Cor. 4:4; Col. 1:15). Paul's understanding of the image of God in humanity is related to our need for God. The image of God has been defaced through human sin, and it must be restored. This restoration comes through contact with the true image, Jesus. This image is potentially present now in believers, but it is to be perfected in the future (2 Cor. 15:49).

INCARNATION. The coming of the eternal Son of God into the world as a human being, Jesus Christ. The term, which literally means "in-flesh-ment," does not appear in the New Testament, but a verbal equivalent occurs in John 1:14, "was made flesh" (KJV).

The term *incarnation* has at least two meanings. It may refer to the moment of the Son's coming, that is, to the virgin birth of Christ; or it may refer to the entirety of his coming, and thus to the person, Jesus Christ.

In the fourth and fifth centuries, the church was challenged to articulate its convictions concerning Jesus Christ. It often employed the Greek word *enanthropopesis* ("in-man-ment") to describe Jesus; he was the Son of God enmanned. The proper language for speaking of him was worked out by the Council of Chalcedon in AD 451; Jesus was one "person" who had two "natures," the divine and the human.

INSPIRATION. God's influence upon the writers of the Bible, which resulted in their writings being the Word of God.

The word *inspiration* means to breathe in. Christians have spoken of their Scriptures as inspired of God, meaning that they are God-breathed. Though there are various ways for understanding the process of inspiration, all Christians agree that the Scriptures are authoritative for faith and practice. Some have understood inspiration to be mechanical; that is, God dictated the words to the writers. Others have understood inspiration in dynamic terms; that is, God worked through the minds and spirits of the writers to convey his message. Second Peter 1:21 maintains that prophets "moved by the Holy Spirit spoke from God." Second Timothy 3:16, which is the only passage of Scripture which uses the word *inspiration*, affirms that all Scripture is given by inspiration of God; it may also be translated, "Every scripture inspired by God is authoritative." The meaning here clearly is that God gives life to words of Scripture, just as Adam had life breathed into him in the Garden of Eden. The writers of the Bible used their rational faculties (1 Cor. 7:25). They wrote for a variety of purposes, among them to encourage, to warn, to record history, and to inspire.

The Old Testament is understood by Christians to be the background for the Christian gospel concerning Christ. All the Scriptures are to be understood and interpreted in the light of Christ. That the Bible is inspired does not prevent Christians from reading it analytically. On the contrary, they have the responsibility of trying to understand what it meant in its own day as well as what it means today.

Controversies concerning the inspiration of the Scripture have been frequent in the nineteenth and twentieth centuries. We do not know precisely how God inspired the Scriptures, though we can emphatically affirm that he did inspire them. The Scriptures have proven themselves to be authentic by their usefulness and power. The key question about the Scriptures is: are the Scriptures authoritative, that is, are they normative for the individual Christian and for the church?

Obviously the inspiration of Scripture would have been of no value to us today if the Scripture had not been preserved over centuries and translated into our language and read by us. Because this is such a complicated process—writing, copying, preserving, translating, and reading—one must accept by faith

---

that God can speak to us today through the Bible. For those who have exercised such faith, the Bible has proven itself to be trustworthy.

J

JESUS CHRIST. A first-century Jew who also was the Son of God, the Founder and Lord of the church, who by his death and resurrection provided salvation for humanity.

Historians who seek to learn about Jesus' life must depend largely upon the New Testament, though there are corroborative statements in some ancient writers such as Pliny the Younger and Tacitus. The basic events of Jesus' life are better attested than most from the ancient world. He was born in Palestine during the reign of Augustus; he conducted a public ministry of preaching and healing during the reign of Tiberius; he called a small group of followers; he incurred the wrath of established religion; he was executed by crucifixion at the hands of the Romans when Pontius Pilate was procurator of Judea; shortly thereafter some of his followers proclaimed that he had been raised from the dead; out of their preaching grew the Christian church, which began as a small Jewish sect, became an independent religion, and dominated the Roman Empire within four centuries, and today comprises almost a third of the earth's population.

These bare historical facts, however, conceal the deeper meaning of Jesus as perceived by Christians. The church has been led to that deeper, theological, and religious meaning in two ways. First, Jesus was raised from the dead by the Father. This confirmed his teachings and validated his ministry. The resurrection also was a saving act of God which inaugurated a new era in the relations of God and people. Second, and very closely tied to the first, the community of faith experienced the salvation Jesus provided and felt themselves to be living in the new era. In brief, Jesus was the Savior. But how was the new community to understand and to express its faith in Jesus as the Savior?

The New Testament provides large numbers of expressions of the religious meaning of Jesus. They are mostly oriented to Jewish life, since the earliest church was Jewish. For example, they said that Jesus was the Christ (Acts 2:36). This meant that he was the *anointed* or chosen person through whom God had brought his salvation. They said that he was superior to all earlier prophets and leaders, that he was superior to the law, and that his death upon the cross was superior to all the sacrifices provided through the law (Heb.) They said that he had existed before the world and that he participated in the creation of the world (Col. 1:15-20). They said he was the Word of God made flesh (John 1:1-14). This meant, among other things, that he was the fullest revelation of the character and purpose of God and that through him God had spoken. In these and other ways, the Christian community confessed the profound religious significance of Jesus.

But in doing so, the church has tried also to confess the true humanity of Jesus Christ. Thus the New Testament describes him as a Jewish man of Palestine during the Roman occupation, as a person who was born, who grew up into a youth and then a man, who had flesh and blood, who experienced sorrow and pain, who struggled with and overcame temptations, who served God obediently, and who finally died in a manner appropriate for the worst criminals. It explicity condemns those who deny that Jesus had a human body (1 John 4:1-3).

Nor did the Bible imply in its affirmation of his transcendent, divine dimension, and in its affirmation of his true, real, human dimension that he was two persons. Not a scrap of evidence exists to suggest that the writers of the New Testament ever considered Jesus anything other than one person. Even language which we today feel is acceptable, which says "As God he did this and as man he did that," does not occur in the New Testament. The New Testament does not defend, or even affirm, the unity of Jesus; it simply everywhere assumes it and nowhere employs any phrase which might erode it.

These, then, are the basic data of the New Testament

concerning Jesus: he is divine; he is human; he is one person. What else, one might ask, needs to be said theologically?

The theological understanding of Jesus did develop after the close of the New Testament for several important reasons. First, it was necessary to translate the Jewish ways of speaking about Jesus into terms meaningful to Gentiles. This was not always easy. The term *Christ*, for example, was meaningless to Gentiles who did not cherish a hope that God would send an anointed deliverer. The result was that it came to be used as a name rather than a title, not unlike the way many surnames in English had their beginnings as titles or vocations (King, Carpenter, Miller, Shoemaker, Smith).

Second, Christology developed as new questions were asked which had not been asked or answered in the New Testament. For example, did Jesus have a human soul? This question was asked by Apollinarius in the fourth century, and the church responded that Jesus did (this answer is found in the Nicene Creed which probably was drawn up at the Council of Constantinople in AD 381).

Third, Christology developed as the church assimilated more fully the meaning of the New Testament. It is one thing to formally affirm a truth and quite another thing to internalize it, take it into your heart, appreciate it deeply, and allow it to have its full weight. This happened in the nineteenth century concerning the humanity of Christ. As a new understanding of history developed, the church learned to appreciate in a new way the reality of Jesus' humanity. Sometimes, unfortunately, this was done at the expense of Jesus' deity, as in liberalism, but at other times it was done by those who maintained the full deity of Christ. This led to a realistic, true, and profound understanding of Jesus.

Finally, Christology develops for the very good reason that, since people love Jesus so much, they are bound to go on thinking about him and trying to understand him. That is what we do toward those we truly love, and it is a very good practice. As is seen in sermons, hymns, books, and personal confessions, individual Christians continue to grow "in the . . . knowledge of . . . Jesus Christ" (2 Pet. 3:18).

We have every reason to suppose that the church will continue to strive to understand Jesus Christ better. Though there is the risk of making mistakes, the effort surely is worthwhile. In the meantime, along with the theological response to Jesus, there are other responses, some much more important: Jesus is called upon as Savior; witness is given concerning Jesus; Jesus is loved and trusted; Jesus is felt as the Companion on life's way; Jesus is worshiped. All of this was true in the New Testament, and presumably it will be true until Jesus completes his work in the final consummation and every knee shall bow to him.

JUDGMENT. The divine appraisal of all human beings.

The Jewish nation functioned as a theocracy; God was the sovereign Lord, and he ruled through the earthly kings. As Lord, God was the Giver of the law, its authorized Interpreter, and its Enforcer. Since he was a righteous God, his judgments were also righteous: he opposed sin and supported the cause of the innocent, however powerless they might be.

Eventually Israel came to look forward to a great day of judgment when all accounts would be settled by the Lord. This was often visualized in what we today would term civil rather than criminal terms: all wrongs would be righted, all relationships manifest. This judgment would be a matter of salvation as well as of condemnation, and it would reveal God's righteousness (we today call this *theodicy*; see Isa. 2:12 to 3:5).

Jesus spoke of himself as a future Judge of people. This role occupies more of Jesus' teaching than is often realized. Perhaps the classic passage is Matthew 25:14-46, which reveals that while his work of judgment involves condemning the wicked (who are surprised at his condemnation) it also includes justifying or saving the righteous (who also are surprised). In speaking of himself as the Judge of the final day, Jesus bore witness to his messianic work and, therefore, to his identity.

The fact that Jesus is the Judge of humanity should provide comfort to some, but trouble others. It answers the question, What is the God like to whom I finally will answer? The God who judges humanity is a God who is gentle, loving, gracious, and compassionate, not a God who is arbitrary or vindictive. On the other hand, those who hate Jesus and his humility and grace and his acceptance of the poor and the outcast should be made uneasy by the recognition that he is to be the final Judge of their lives.

Traditionally, the church has distinguished the particular judgment from the general or final judgment. The particular judgment is a judgment of individuals at the moment of their death, and the final judgment is a judgment of all humanity at the end of history.

JUSTIFICATION. The act of God in Christ by which a person of faith is declared innocent of sin.

This is one of the words used in the New Testament to describe salvation. It is a legal metaphor which presents God as our judge. Because Christ paid the penalty for sin which we deserved, God declares us justified in his sight if we in faith accept Christ's offer of salvation.

The New Testament, and especially Paul, teaches that a person is justified by faith and not by works, that is, by moral worthiness (see Acts 13:39). All people are sinful, and justification is possible only through faith in Jesus Christ who alone is capable of satisfying our debt to God. The result of justification is that we are "created in Christ Jesus for good works" (Eph. 2:10). This process of growing like Christ is called sanctification.

Throughout the history of the church, theologians have found justification and related legal terms useful in their understanding of salvation. In recent years, however, some theologians have become uncomfortable with legal metaphors for salvation. They point out that the relationship between God and people is far more than legal. While this is true, many Christians continue to find the legal metaphors for salvation helpful.

KINGDOM OF GOD. The reign of God over those people who submit themselves in faith to God as sovereign.

The kingdom of God was at the heart of Jesus' teaching and preaching (Mark 1:15). He taught that the kingdom of God (or the kingdom of heaven) is already coming in the world. It was begun with his coming and expands as individuals repent of their sins and by faith accept Christ as Lord and Savior. The kingdom is not yet fully complete but will be completed in the future.

The signs of the kingdom of God were manifest in Jesus' miracles. When John the Baptist asked from prison if Jesus were the Messiah, Jesus responded by pointing to his healing miracles (Luke 7:22). The ultimate demonstration that God was at work in Christ was his resurrection. It was the signal that a new kingdom was at hand. Further demonstrations include the establishment of the church at Pentecost, the growth and continuation of the church through the centuries, and the transformation of lives through the proclamation of the gospel.

In the teaching of Jesus, the kingdom of God was God's work and not ours. This does not mean that we have no part in the kingdom. On the contrary, Christians are responsible for proclaiming it. Since it has not yet been fully realized, every Christian is to pray, as Jesus taught, that the kingdom will come in all its fullness (Matt. 6:9-10).

LAITY. Christians who are not ordained as ministers.

The word *laity* means *people*. In the Christian church, it has come to mean those who are not ordained as ministers. The Bible does not teach a two-tiered structure within the life of the church. It does teach that God gives different gifts to believers and that these gifts are to be used for the building up of the people of God (1 Cor. 12:4 *ff.*). Some Christians are called by God to use their gifts as leaders of the church. These individuals are ordained to the ministry by the church as a recognition of God's call. They have no special privileges in the church but rather are to be servants of the church (Rom. 11:3 *ff.*). The word *laity* has come to mean nonprofessional, and many Christians refuse to discover, develop, or use their gifts because they are not ordained. This is a misunderstanding of the call to ministry. All Christians have gifts and are responsible for their use and development.

LAW. The commands of God as found in the Old Testament and especially the Ten Commandments.

The Mosaic law was the heart of the Jewish faith after the Exodus. The people of Israel understood it as God's pattern for personal and corporate living. It included commands concerning both moral behavior and ritual practices. When the law was originally given, obedience to it was Israel's way of showing appreciation to God for his deliverance and covenant love. Obedience to the law soon came to be a means of securing and ensuring God's blessing for individuals and for the nation (Ps. 119).

In the New Testament, the law of Moses was still seen to be true and vital; but because no one could fulfill it, it was self-defeating in nature. The law stood as an ultimate condemnation of people. The New Testament teaches that Christ made provision for our forgiveness by God. He did this by completely fulfilling the law; he lived a sinless life. Christ also supplemented the law by teaching the deeper moral truths of the law (Matt. 5:17-48). He also did something which the law could never do; he provided as a free gift the righteousness which the law had demanded of people (Rom. 8:3-4).

Christians now have the responsibility of interpreting the law in the light of Christ (Rom. 10:4). Since he did not come to destroy the law but to fulfill it (Matt. 5:17-18), Christians must seek for the essence of the law of the Old Testament. Though many of the ritual practices of the Old Testament no longer apply in the Christian era, the law of Christ is the fulfillment of the deeper intentions of God for his people (Matt. 22:34-40).

LORD'S SUPPER. An ordinance of the church in which Christ's death is symbolized and remembered in the form of a meal.

The Lord's Supper, along with baptism, is one of two ordinances which Jesus instituted. At the Last Supper, he commanded his disciples to continue to share in a meal observance "in remembrance" of him (1 Cor. 11:24). This meal of bread and cup is also referred to as the Eucharist, the Mass, or Communion. The meal is a symbol of Christ's sacrificial death. The broken bread symbolizes his body, and the cup symbolizes his blood.

Roman Catholics speak of this act as a sacrifice. The bread and cup are transformed into Christ's body and blood, and by participating in the sacrament one receives a special grace or power from God. It is necessary, therefore, for a Catholic regularly to participate in the Mass in order to continue to receive God's grace.

Evangelicals have insisted that Christ is present at the meal but that the meal is a remembrance service which eloquently proclaims the gospel. As a result Evangelicals tend to celebrate the Lord's Supper less often than Roman Catholics so that the symbolism will not be lost by repetition. Also, Evangelicals have a table in their churches, which speaks of the meal, rather than an altar, which would speak of a sacrifice. Furthermore, Roman Catholic laypeople receive only the bread at the service, whereas in Evangelical churches everyone receives both bread and cup.

There are a number of areas concerning the Lord's Supper where Christians disagree: who should participate; in what sense Christ is present; the attitude participants should have; and whether the meal should be served only by those who are ordained. All these controversies are made to seem insignificant by Christ's command to "do this in remembrance of me."

LOVE. Devotion to another person. When you love someone, you want to be with him and you act in his best interests.

Love is the central attribute of God. The Old Testament speaks in dramatic ways of God as loving his people by acting to create them, by making them his own, by patiently being with them in their failures.

The New Testament records that "God is love" (1 John 4:8). Because God loves the world, he has sent Jesus to bring life to humanity (John 3:16). Jesus himself summarized God's commands in terms of love: love God (from Deut. 6:5) and love your neighbor (Lev. 19:18; see Matt. 22:34-40). His life was characterized by actions, especially toward outcasts and others, of such a nature that he was the embodiment of divine love and grace. Paul's great hymn to love (1 Cor. 13) may be read as a description of the character of Jesus.

It, therefore, is understandable that love has the central place in Christian ethics. God's Spirit works to create love in the people of God (Gal. 5:22). People who have been loved by God ought naturally to love him in return (1 John 4:19), and to love one another as well (1 John 4:11). Apart from love, God's purpose of creating a community of his people would not succeed; therefore, love is an indispensable ingredient in God's eternal purpose.

Love is not sentimental; in fact, it is not fundamentally an emotion at all, but a way of living and acting. The love of God is not expressed merely in terms of his feelings toward humanity but also in terms of his actions: "God shows his love for us in that while we are yet sinners Christ died for us" (Rom. 5:8). The same is true of the human love which is a response to God's love; fundamentally it is a way of acting, not a manner of feeling. Love for God takes the form of obedience: if we love him, we will keep his commands (see John 14:15; 15:9-17). Love for others takes the form of service: if we love the hungry, we will feed them; if we love the lonely, we will visit them.

That is why love can be commanded; feelings cannot be commanded (we are not always responsible for how we feel), but behavior can, and love is a style of behavior.

That is also why there are in the Bible rules and principles for living. The difference between a love ethic and a rule ethic dissolves when love is understood as a manner of living more than a matter of feeling, for rules and principles provide guidance for the person who sets out to live a life of love.

MAN. The created being who has the capacity to relate to God in personal terms.

The key affirmation in the Bible concerning humanity is that *"in the image of God created he him; male and female created he them,"* (Gen. 1:27, authors' italics). Though there is no consensus about what this means, it is certain that this affirmation is meant to distinguish man from the rest of creation.

The identification of God with humanity was made clear in the incarnation. In a way that we cannot explain, God became man in the person of Jesus of Nazareth. As a result, God experienced what it means to be a human being.

The question which our existence, as well as the incarnation, raises is, "What is man"? (Ps. 8:4). Though the answers to this question vary widely among religious and nonreligious people, there are some accepted generalizations. For example, it is agreed that to be human is to live within the confines of space and time. For Christians, the key to understanding human existence is to be found in relationship to God as revealed in Jesus Christ.

This relationship began with the creation of man and woman whom God calls "good" (Gen. 1:31). Subsequently, God blessed the marriage relationship (Gen. 2:24; Matt. 19:5-6), the procreation of children (Gen. 1:28), and meaningful work (Gen. 2:15). The relationship which God intended to have with humanity was spoiled by human sin (Gen. 3:1-24). The purpose of God as it is revealed in Scripture is to restore that relationship. God has chosen to achieve that end by loving us rather than through force or manipulation. It is God's greatest compliment to his creation that he respects human freedom and will not compel people to obey and love him. The New Testament describes Jesus as the "new man." Just as Adam symbolizes human failure, Jesus symbolizes humanity at its best. Not only is Jesus our example but he is also our Savior. He saves us from the destructiveness of our own sin and frees us from our bondage to it.

Through our relationship with Jesus, God transforms us into his likeness when we willingly place ourselves in submission to him. Through that process we may become all we were created to be—creatures made in the image of God.

Though each person is an individual, he or she is not meant to live a solitary life (Gen. 2:18). We are meant to live in a community, but our sin prevents us from loving our neighbors just as it prevents us from loving God. The creation of the nation of Israel, God's promise to always preserve the faithful, and his establishment of the church all bear testimony to God's purpose of creating community.

Our greatest enemy is death (Ps. 49:10-14). Though apart from God he is not immortal, man may gain eternal life through a relationship with God in Christ (1 Cor. 15:57). The resurrection of Jesus gives us hope for life after death. That hope is nourished by the presence of Christ in the life of the Christian.

MARRIAGE. The lifelong commitment of a man and a woman to live together in the establishment of a family.

Marriage was the first institution established by God (Gen. 2:21-24). This commitment is sanctified by God, and it is sealed with physical intercourse: "a man leaves his father and mother and joins himself to his wife, and they become one body" (Gen. 2:24, authors' translation). Jesus added to this definition a solemn injunction, "so then what God has united, man must not divide" (Matt. 19:6, authors' translation).

In the Old Testament, women were viewed as property. Therefore, marriage relationships were not egalitarian. Women could be divorced quite easily but had no right to divorce their husbands. Jesus spoke to this issue and declared that all divorces are contrary to the will of God (Mark 10:11-12).

In the New Testament, a new standard for marriage was introduced. Paul likened the marriage relationship to the relationship of Christ and the church (Eph. 5:21-33). He also taught the necessity of mutual submission: "be subject to one another out of reverence for Christ" (Eph. 5:21).

Though procreation is not the rationale for marriage, it is a blessing which flows from it. The bearing, rearing, and nurturing of children is one of humanity's greatest responsibilities.

MILLENNIUM. A thousand-year reign of Christ.

Although the millennium is mentioned in only one passage in the Bible (Rev. 20:1-10), and although that passage occurs in a book which contains many metaphors and other figures of speech, Protestant theologies are often appraised in terms of their stance toward the millennium. Is the millennium a literal reign of Christ upon earth? Or does it represent an age in which the message of Christ wins the hearts of most, or even all, of the world? If Christ returns to earth physically, does he do so before the thousand years, in order to inaugurate it (premillenialism), or does he return after people have created a thousand years of peace and love (postmilennialism)?

Christians have debated the millennium and other aspects of the future of human history for centuries. There has never been a universal consensus about the details of the future. Presumably the debate will continue in the future. Perhaps the wisest thing is to affirm that the future of the planet is in the hands of God who "in His own time and in His way, will bring the world to its appropriate end" (*The Baptist Faith and Message*). Scholars may wish to debate the details, but that affirmation is what is essential for the day-to-day faith and life of most Christians.

MINISTRY. The collective name for all the acts of service which the community of faith performs in response to God's call. Although the church is sometimes perceived as a self-serving institution, which unfortunately it sometimes is, its true nature is the opposite. It is a community whose reason for being is to serve God by serving others.

The example for the church's service is its Lord and Master, Jesus Christ, who "came not to be ministered unto, but to minister" (Mark 10:45, KJV). The motive for the church's ministry is love. The resources for its ministry are the gifts which God's Spirit distributes to the church.

Christian ministry is carried out both by individuals and by the community acting together. Although certain individuals are called *ministers* within the church (as they were in the New Testament, for example, 2 Cor. 3:6), in an important sense all Christians are ministers, that is, persons who do acts of service to others in Christ's name. Paradoxically, the greatest Christians are those who serve (Mark 10:43-44). Likewise, the entire church can be said to be a minister, for its goal is to serve the world in Jesus' name.

Various analyses of ministry have been employed. For example, some ministries are large (such as the operation of a great hospital), and some small (the giving of a cup of cold water). Again, some are named in the New Testament ("the word of wisdom," 1 Cor. 12:8, KJV) and others are not (the ministry of pastoral counseling, for example). Some are public and visible, such as the ministry of mass evangelism; others are private and inconspicuous, such as gifts of charity to the needy.

MIRACLES. Supernatural acts of God.

Since Christians believe that God created the world, they do not find it difficult to affirm that God can intervene in the course of history with special acts which contravene the natural laws. In one sense these laws themselves are supernatural since they were established by divine decree.

Within the scope of history, Christians claim that there have been a number of miraculous acts. In the Old Testament, the deliverance of Israel from Egypt is portrayed in that way. God forced the Egyptians to let his people go. He protected them from their pursuers. He provided for their needs in the wilderness and ensured their conquest of the Promised Land. These acts were not arbitrary, but purposeful. God was establishing a people he intended to use in the salvation of humanity.

This same purpose is evident in the miracles of Jesus who refused to use miracles for his own purposes but used them only to glorify God (Matt. 4:1-10). The ultimate miracle in Jesus' life is the resurrection. It is a sign to people that God is in control of the universe and that Jesus is the One through whom he is providing salvation.

Since every miracle is open to some other explanation, it must be concluded that a belief in the miraculous is an act of faith. It is in this sense that the New Testament speaks of miracles as signs which point people to God (Matt. 11:1-6).

MISSIONS. The work which Jesus Christ, as the Lord of the church, assigns (commissions) his people to do.

The etymology of the word *mission* (Latin, *missio*) and of the word *apostle* (Greek, *apostello*) is identical and means *sent out*. Jesus sent out his church (Matt. 28:19), so that the church cannot be the church if it remains within its own buildings. To be the church and to obey its Lord, it must go out into the world.

From its inception, therefore, Christianity has been a missionary religion, the first religion to attempt to win all mankind to its faith and life. The Book of Acts records the story of the early church learning the worldwide scope of its message (see Jesus' programmatic words in Acts 1:8). The greatest missionary of all time may have been the apostle Paul; but tens of thousands of others have felt God's Spirit leading them out into the world, and many have served Christ heroically. The success of the work of these missionaries may be gauged by the fact that today just under 33 percent of the people of the earth profess faith in Jesus Christ. On the other hand, vast numbers of people live and die without ever meeting a Christian, let alone having a serious opportunity to respond to the gospel.

The church fulfills its mission in two ways. First, it organizes itself and sends out, in a formal sense, missionaries. Also, each Christian is to think of himself or herself as *sent out* by Christ into the community, school, office, and so on, to be a bearer of the good news of Jesus Christ.

The primary work of missions must be the proclamation of the gospel, but this does not exhaust the missionary work. Evangelism must be followed by Christian teaching and nurture and by all the acts of worship and service which characterized the early church and, indeed, which the early church learned from its ultimate pattern, the life of Jesus Christ.

N

NEW BIRTH. The act of God by which a sinner is graciously accepted and transformed into a child of God.

From the beginning, the church recognized not only the continuity of Jesus Christ with the Old Testament but also the newness of God's work in Christ. A new age was inaugurated in Christ, and a new covenant was made by Jesus' blood; followers of Christ became new creations, and God put a new heart and a new spirit within them. The old things had passed away, and the new had arrived (2 Cor. 5:17).

The new birth (John 3:1-15; 1 Pet. 1:3-5), or regeneration (Titus 3:3-7), is a part of God's new work through Jesus Christ. It is God's gift of life to those who were dead in sins (Eph. 2:1-10). It is entirely an act of God, for no one can cause himself to be born anew. It is entirely an act of grace, for no one deserves the gift of God's life. And it is entirely a successful act, for those to whom life is given do become and remain children of the Heavenly Father.

Because the new birth is associated with water in the New Testament (John 3; Titus 3), the church has often taught that the new birth occurs at the moment of baptism. Baptists and others have objected to this identification, arguing that it is ritualistic and arbitrary and undermines the graciousness of God's regenerating work. When baptism is performed in the ancient manner of immersion, it pictures vividly the inner experience of the child of God who has died to the old way of life and been born again to a new way of life.

The new birth is fundamentally God's act, so it is not appropriate to suggest that it will be experienced in identical ways by all who receive it. It may or may not be an emotional experience, and usually it does not involve mystical elements. What may be said, on the authority of the Bible, is that this great and free gift will be given to all who put their trust in Jesus Christ.

ORDINANCES. Baptism and the Lord's Supper are called ordinances because Jesus Christ explicitly ordained that they should be observed by his disciples (Matt. 28:19-20; 26:26-29).

In Roman Catholic theology, there are seven sacraments, including baptism and the Eucharist (Lord's Supper). The word *sacrament* is derived from a Latin word (*sacramentum*) which was used to translate the New Testament word *mystery (mysterion)*, found in passages such as Colossians 1:2. The other five sacraments are confirmation, marriage, ordination, confession and penance, and extreme unction. Even in Roman Catholic theology, baptism and the Eucharist are regarded as the major sacraments, and the other five are lower in rank.

Baptism and the Lord's Supper differ from the other five in two ways. First, Christ specifically ordained these two but not the others (Catholic theologians sometimes claim that he ordained the others, but the New Testament does not support this). Second, baptism and the Lord's Supper are pictures of the death and resurrection of Christ; baptism portrays this as a person is immersed in water and then comes forth; in the Lord's Supper the broken bread portrays Christ's broken body, and the cup portrays Christ's blood. The other five Catholic sacraments do not portray the gospel events.

Neither does footwashing which is mentioned in John 13.

For this reason, and also because there is no record in Acts or the Epistles to indicate that the church ever practiced footwashing as a rite, it has never been regarded as a sacrament.

Of the seven sacraments in Roman Catholic theology, Protestants usually practice either four or five, omitting extreme unction, confession-penance, and sometimes, confirmation. Some Protestants, such as Quakers and the Salvation Army, practice no ordinances, believing that all that is important is the spiritual meaning of baptism and the Lord's Supper.

ORDINATION. The practice by which the community of faith sets apart certain persons for special kinds of ministry.

Virtually all religions have ceremonies by which they set apart individuals for religious duties. Leviticus 8 describes how Moses ordained Aaron and his sons to the priesthood.

The great precedent for Christian ordination is Jesus' call and commissioning of the twelve (Matt. 10:1 to 11:1). These twelve (except for Judas) exercised leadership in the church after Christ's ascension. The church set apart for service various persons (Acts 6:1-6; 13:1-3). Though the entire ordination service is not described, it seems to have included both fasting and the laying on of hands. In the Pastoral Epistles, laying on of hands was involved in setting apart a person for ministry (2 Tim. 1:6).

Roman Catholic and Protestant churches differ concerning the administration and significance of ordination. Roman Catholic theology teaches that ordination is performed by an ordained person (today, a bishop), who is thereby passing along a grace and authority that goes back to Christ (apostolic succession). Protestant theology generally teaches that the church has been given authority by Christ, and the church ordains through its ministers. Roman Catholic theology emphasizes that the major gift received at ordination is the gift to consecrate the host in the Eucharist; in fact, at ordination the new priest conducts the celebration of the Eucharist for the first time. Protestant theology emphasizes that the major ministry to which one is ordained is the ministry of the Word. The ordinand often receives a Bible as a symbol of this emphasis.

All Christians agree that the church's responsibility is not to call persons to ministry, but to recognize God's call to a person and to confirm that call by the rite of ordination. Ordination, therefore, is an ecclesial activity which does not initiate but rather responds to the prior call of God. A major part of the burden of the church is to be sensitive enough to recognize God's calling in the lives of individual Christians.

Some Christians object to the practice of ordination in principle, pointing out that the distinction between laity and clergy can become pernicious, that all Christians have a call to ministry, and that the New Testament does not contain clear and formal examples of and instructions for ordination. These observations are true. It is a healthy thing for the church to emphasize the responsibility of all Christians to minister, as has been done in the lay renewal movement of the twentieth century. Even so, Christ did set aside the twelve in a special sense, and the early church did ordain Paul and others for special work. Affirming the responsibility of all Christians need not require the denial of the special call which God gives to certain individuals.

ORTHODOXY. Theology which adheres to the authority of the Bible and the traditional teachings of the church.

Though there is no explicit creed in the New Testament, Christians have maintained through the centuries a tradition which expresses the essential features of the Christian faith. These features include belief in the Triune nature of God, the authority of the Scriptures, the person and work of Christ, the reality of the church, the value of baptism and the Lord's Supper, the second coming of Christ, and the final judgment.

Though there may be varying interpretations of this tradition, none of these features could be eliminated in any orthodox expression of Christianity. Such deviation would be heresy. However, Christians through the centuries have always affirmed that these expressions of the faith are human attempts to describe the reality that lies behind and transcends human description. Christians have the responsibility for maintaining the faith (1 Tim. 6:3) and for teaching it clearly (2 Tim. 1:13-14).

P

PASTOR. The spiritual leader of a local Christian congregation.

The word *pastor* means shepherd. It is the responsibility of the pastor to care for his flock, the local congregation. This is not a vocation that a person chooses rather it is given to a person as a calling from God (Acts 20:28).

The pattern for this ministry is to be found in the ministry of Jesus who called himself "the good shepherd" (John 10:11) and who understood his ministry as one of service (Mark 10:45). Thus the pastor is not an authority so much as he is a servant. He has the responsibility of "feeding the sheep" (see John 21:16). This is done through preaching, teaching, administering the ordinances, and ministering to the other needs of the people. The pastor is responsible to God for the administration of the church which entails teaching, comforting, and leading the people (1 Cor. 14:3). Like all the leaders of the church the pastor is to use his gifts "to equip God's people for work in his service, to the building up of the body of Christ" (Eph. 4:12, NEB).

PEACE. The sense of contentment which comes from being rightly related to God.

Peace can mean absence of war in the Bible, but its primary meaning has to do with one's spiritual condition. The Hebrew word *shalom* signified wholeness or unity. It describes the state of one's life when each aspect of one's life was in its proper relationship to everything else (Ps. 29:11).

In the New Testament, the corresponding word was *eirene*. It carries the same meaning as *shalom* and is a frequent theme of the New Testament writers. Jesus' assurances to his disciples involved a promise of peace: "Peace is my parting gift to you, my own peace, such as the world cannot give" (John 14:27, NEB).

The peace which Jesus promised is predicated on one's having proper relationships. Primarily this involves having a relationship with Jesus (Col. 1:19-20). The proclamation of Jesus is the message which when heard and accepted forms the foundation for true peace (Acts 10:36).

Christians build upon this foundation by resolving internal conflicts within their lives. Jesus pointed out that we cannot be rightly related to others unless we are at peace with ourselves (Mark 12:31). The way to personal peace is found through our relationship to Christ. When he rules in our hearts, we can be at peace with ourselves (Col. 3:15).

This internal peace should result in proper relationships with others. Jesus encouraged his followers to be peacemakers (Matt. 5:9). For Christians there is a special need to "be at peace" among ourselves (1 Thess. 5:13); however, we also are responsible for "living peaceably with all men" (Rom. 12:18, KJV).

Jesus never promised his disciples that they would avoid conflict by following him. On the contrary, he knew his mission would bring more divisions than it would harmony (Luke 12:51). However, Jesus did promise his disciples that in their relationship to him they would find peace (John 16:33). Paul wrote that Jesus is our peace, that Jesus made peace, and that Jesus preached peace (Eph. 2:14-15,17).

PERSON, PERSONAL. A human being; like a human being.

One of the most fundamental of all distinctions is the distinction between the personal and nonpersonal in the world. The distinction is not innate but must be learned. Mistakes may be made, as when a child treats a toy as a person. Even so, the distinction is a fundamental one and guides the thinking of most persons.

It is a vital distinction for religion. The Jewish-Christian religion has always affirmed that God is personal. Indeed, this is true of most of the world religions. The Old Testament does use nonpersonal metaphors for God, such as "God is our refuge and strength" (Ps. 46:1), but these are understood as secondary to the more fundamental, personal character of God. Thus, the meaning of Psalm 46:1 is not that God is fundamentally like a refuge, and we personify the refuge; it is rather that God is fundamentally like a person, who protects us as a refuge does.

The personal understanding of God is fundamental. To speak of God as personal is to use a metaphor; all understandings of God are metaphors, for God transcends all human experience. What is being affirmed with this metaphor is that, given the distinction between persons and nonpersons, God is more like the persons.

Since we are persons, we have an inside knowledge of what it is to be persons. This makes it difficult to analyze the constituent elements which go together to make up a person. Yet an effort must be made if we are to say more than that a person is whatever is not a nonperson. Traditionally the discussion of what is essential to personal life has been carried on in terms of the soul and of the image of God.

A working definition of a person might include the following: a person is a rational, free, moral, valuing, self-conscious, subject who is influenced by history, culture, and a subconscious life or memory, whose active and passive experiences are mediated through a body in space and time, and who is capable of entering into a relationship of love with another person or persons, and thus of being a member of a community. This definition includes thirteen relevant factors for understanding a person; there may be others. Any effort to define a person without these factors would seem to be incomplete. Even these factors are problematic. For example, if self-consciousness is essential to personhood, does one cease to be a person when one is asleep or in a coma? Again, if appreciation of moral and other values is essential to personhood, is an infant less than personal? If being a person involves all the factors, in what sense is a person a unity, a whole? These questions and others arise from within the community of faith. From the outside world other questions come. For example, are human beings really free? Is there a self? Are the rational processes dependable? Is love an illusion?

The Christian faith does not supply the answers to all the mystery which surrounds personhood. What it does do is to affirm the highest possible estimate of personal life: human beings are made in God's own image. It does this, not by sentimental, wishful thinking, but in the face of the most vivid awareness of humanity's fallenness and sinfulness. In that sense, Christianity offers the most optimistic view of human life.

PRAYER. Talking to God who listens and responds because he loves.

Prayers are a part of all religions; people have prayed for as long as they have been on earth. In the Old Testament prayers were constantly offered to God; the Psalms are prayers (and hymns) offered to God. Jesus spoke frequently about prayer; he encouraged private prayer, warned against attempting to impress God by effusive language, and gave his disciples a model (Matt. 6:5-13). He himself addressed God with the intimate term *Abba* (Daddy), and he taught his followers also to call God "Our Father." Today this way of addressing God may seem obviously proper, but it was not obvious when Jesus originated it. It suggested that Jesus felt himself to be in a uniquely intimate relationship with God, and he then introduced his followers to a similarly close relationship with God.

Christian prayer is not a form of magic, not an incantation which in itself alters the world. It is talking to God who alters the world, sometimes in response to prayers.

Christian prayer is not an effort to coerce God into certain actions. It recognizes God's freedom, his freedom to say no even to the most sincere prayer.

Does prayer really make a difference? It does, but not because of its sincerity or intensity, or any other quality in itself. It makes a difference for one reason: God in his grace has chosen to be attentive to the prayers of human beings.

The most obvious kind of prayer is one which makes requests of God, either on behalf of oneself (petition) or of others (intercession). Such requests are perfectly appropriate, having been encouraged by Jesus (Matt. 7:7-12). It is inevitable that human requests will reflect human concerns, just as the requests a child makes of his parents will reflect his childish concerns. A good parent will respect the childish concerns of her children, but will look forward to a time when the children grow up and share her adult concerns. Likewise, God wants his children to become mature and to share his divine purposes. Requests which do this are what is meant by praying according to God's will. The most Christian request is, therefore, "Thy kingdom come, Thy will be done" (Matt. 6:10).

There are five other kinds of prayer besides requests. They are worship, thanksgiving, confession of sin, commitment of life, and asking questions of God. The first four of these are clear and require no explanation. Perhaps it should be said that worship is the ultimate kind of prayer. The fifth kind of prayer, asking questions, is widespread in the Bible; an example is Psalm 74:1: "O God, why dost thou cast us off for ever?/Why does thy anger smoke against the sheep of thy pasture?" God is able to hear the deepest questions of the human heart with love and understanding.

Prayers may be said privately or publicly; both are appropriate, though the warnings of Jesus about the danger of public prayers should be borne in mind. Prayers may be either formal or informal, though they should never be overly familiar, for it is the Lord God who is being addressed. They may be either spontaneous or prepared. Since the Bible includes many written prayers, it is inappropriate to disregard their value. However, when written prayers are used, it should be with attentiveness and not as an empty ritual.

Some Christians report that they have experienced a kind of prayer which is more advanced and spiritual than the kind described above, talking to God. It is sometimes described as wordless prayer; its traditional name is *mysticism* (from a word meaning to be silent). This kind of prayer has special attraction for people who are interested in meditation and in altered states of consciousness. It is no good saying that consciousness cannot be altered; it can, both with and without the use of drugs. Meditation has a long and honorable history understood either as being quiet and tranquil or as intense concentration. The claims of mystics cannot be shown to be false.

A judgment on these concerns inevitably reflects the ultimate concerns of the person who judges. The present writers would not deny the reality of mysticism, meditation, or altered consciousness; nor would they deny that there is good to be found in these. However, they would affirm two things. First, the ultimate possibility for any human life is love. Love is not self-centered; it is a conscious, freely chosen relationship with another person. To the extent that mysticism, meditation, and altered consciousness do not enhance and enrich the movements of love, they can be no more than a quest for an inferior value. Second, wordless meditation must never supplant spoken prayers. Meditation may or may not be helpful for human life, but prayer certainly is and should never be omitted. "I desire then that in every place the men should pray" (1 Tim. 2:8).

PREACHING. The public proclamation of Christian beliefs and practice.

Preaching finds its precedent in the work of the prophets who proclaimed God's word at his instructions (Jonah 3:2). John the Baptist continued this tradition by preaching in the wilderness of the necessity for repentance (Luke 3:3). This pattern was also adopted by Jesus whose first public act of ministry was preaching (Mark 1:14-15). The Sermon on the Mount is the best-known preaching of Jesus (Matt. 5—7). Jesus sent his early disciples on a preaching mission (Matt. 10:5-7). This preaching tradition was continued in the early church with the first sermon by Peter at Pentecost (Acts 2:14 *ff.*).

The earliest sermons of the church as recorded in Acts had some common elements. This common message was called the *kerygma,* or proclamation. It always included the following affirmations: that the age of fulfillment has come in the person of Jesus and is evidenced by his life, death, and resurrection; that after the resurrection Jesus went to sit at the right hand of the Father; that the Holy Spirit in the church is the sign of Christ's present power and glory; that the messianic age will end with Christ's return; that personal repentance is necessary for salvation; and that the Christian has the promise of forgiveness, the Holy Spirit's presence, and eternal salvation.

The apostle Paul was also a preacher and understood the

proclamation of the gospel to be a privilege and a mandate (Gal. 1:11-12). He understood the Christian message to be a saving proclamation: "It was God's good pleasure through the fullness of the thing preached to save them that believe" (1 Cor. 1:21, authors' translation). Thus the modern preacher is reminded that what matters in preaching is not the preacher but the message preached. That message is to be the good news of Christ.

The purposes of preaching are varied and include: to inform, convict, inspire, motivate, and so on. No preaching is Christian which does not have the gospel as its foundation and the building of the kingdom as its goal (Gal. 1:8-9).

Sermons take a number of forms; expository, topical, and narrative are the well-known forms. It is assumed that all these forms are informed by the biblical witness. The earliest Christian preaching, as we find it in Acts, took a variety of forms depending on the situation and the audience.

The preacher is responsible for the proclamation of the gospel. But the Holy Spirit enables the hearer to perceive the Word of God in the message of the preacher (2 Cor. 3:14-18). Because this continues to happen in the life of the church, preaching remains for Evangelicals the central act of worship.

PREDESTINATION. The foreordination of God concerning the salvation of people.

The Bible includes many words related to predestation; God is said to *determine, decree, elect, ordain, choose, foreknow,* and *know.* Each of these words points to God's ordering of events to achieve his purposes. This is consistent with the biblical claim that God is all-powerful and all-wise and is at work in the world to redeem it. This aspect of God's nature is especially prominent in the Old Testament (Isa. 42:6; Ex. 3:13-17).

In the New Testament, *predestination* is used to describe God's sovereign will to save people (Heb. 9:15; 1 Pet. 1:1; Rom. 8:28-30). This emphasis is not intended to deny human freedom to accept or reject salvation but rather is an affirmation of God's desire to offer salvation to all. If predestination is understood to mean that we have no choice in the matter of our salvation, then Christianity dissolves into determinism. The many passages of Scripture which point to the necessity of personal decision for salvation make this interpretation impossible.

God is at work in the life of each person before he becomes a Christian, but this work of grace does not force that person to accept the gospel. It is in this sense that Christians have given God the credit for their own act of faith. Likewise, if anyone rejects Christ, he alone is responsible for his fate. God has not predestined anyone's rejection. If he had, then people would not be guilty of their own sin.

We who are Christians have been called by God. This calling gives us the assurance of salvation and enables us to serve him (Eph. 2:8-10).

PRIESTHOOD OF THE BELIEVER. The teaching that each person is responsible to God for his or her own religious life.

In contrast to the Jewish practice of having priests who intercede on behalf of the people and who interpret the law of God for the people, Christianity affirms that each Christian may intercede for himself and read the Bible for himself. We in effect are our own priests and thus are responsible for our personal relationship to God (1 Peter 2:4-10; Rev. 1:6; 5:10). This affirmation in the New Testament is understood as a fulfillment of the Scripture "you shall be to me a kingdom of priests" (Ex. 19:6).

Among Baptists this teaching has come to mean the right to freedom of conscience. No one may assume God's role as sovereign. No one may prevent a believer's access to God. Each person is responsible for studying and understanding the Bible, as well as engaging God in prayer. This is consistent with the biblical teaching that each person must work out his own salvation (see Phil. 2:12).

PROOFS FOR GOD'S EXISTENCE. Combinations of evidence and argument, discussed by philosophers since before the time of Christ, which are intended to demonstrate that God is real.

The Bible never attempts to prove God's existence; it

assumes that God is real. This is not surprising, since no one in the biblical world doubted the reality of God.

On the other hand, the biblical writers attempted to argue against those doubts which existed among their contemporaries to help them come to the stance of faith. For example, the Old Testament contains an amusing argument against idolatry (Ps. 115). And in his sermon at Pentecost, Peter defended the reality of Christ's resurrection in two ways. First, he said it had been prophesied in the Old Testament; then Peter claimed that he and his friends had witnessed the risen Christ (Acts 2).

From the fact that the biblical writers never attempted to prove the reality of God, some have concluded that such efforts are inappropriate. But since the Bible does contain defenses of other beliefs, this conclusion seems unwarranted.

The traditional proofs are four. They are the ontological, cosmological, teleological, and moral. Since the latter three contain evidence as well as reasoning, they are better designated as arguments than as proofs.

The ontological (from a word meaning being) proof is the most abstract of the four. Its purest form was originated by Anselm in the twelfth century. It begins by defining God as "that than which no greater (more perfect) can be conceived." It proceeds to argue that a being which exists not only in one's mind but also in reality is greater (more perfect) than one which exists only in one's mind. It concludes that God must, therefore, exist, since it would be a contradiction to say that God is the most perfect being yet exists only in one's mind.

This proof has been convincing to many philosophers since it was first formulated and not convincing to many others. For example, Descartes accepted it, and Kant rejected it. In the twentieth century, its most successful defense and reformulation was by Norman Malcolm. He said that a being may exist either necessarily (it must exist) or contingently (it happens to exist). He thinks that Anselm intended by his definition to rule out both the existence and the nonexistence of God as a contingent matter; either God necessarily exists or he necessarily does not exist. Malcolm then asked what necessary nonexistence would be; it would be a self-contradiction, such as a square circle. Since that is not true of God (there is no contradiction in supposing there is a most perfect being), the only alternative is that God necessarily exists.

The principal objection to this proof is simply that it is not possible to move from an idea (of God) directly to a reality (God).

The second proof, or rather argument, for God's existence is the cosmological (from a word meaning world). It argues that the world is not self-explanatory; it does not create itself; so some self-existing reality behind the world must be responsible for the existence of the world. One rigorous form of the argument is: Since the world exists, either something (God) is eternal or something (the world) came from nothing.

Some Christians have felt that the Bible comes close to this argument when it says, "The heavens declare the glory of God" (Ps. 19:1, KJV) and "God's eternal power and deity are revealed in the things that are created" (Rom. 1:20, authors' translation). However, the biblical writers were not responding to atheists who doubted God's existence. The psalmist reported his experiences of being moved by the heavens to worship God as glorious, and Paul was attempting to show the church at Rome that all people need the salvation which Christ provides.

The third argument is the teleological (from a word meaning purpose). Like the cosmological argument, it begins with the world, in particular with those realities in the world which look as though they were designed for a specific purpose. For example, a human eye looks as though it were designed for seeing. The argument is simply that where there is design, there must be a designer. This is the most popular of the arguments, and it makes a direct and credible appeal to common sense. How could these realities all just happen to function, to work? Surely someone must have designed them.

The major objections to the arguments are two. First, in addition to design in the world, there is a great deal of "un-design"—many pointless things, much waste, many things which make no sense. If the world were designed, couldn't it have been designed better—by omitting cancer, for example, or even mosquitoes? Second, evolution is sometimes offered as a secular explanation for the existence of what appears to be design. Things which work, survive, and over vast ages more and more efficient beings naturally (not supernaturally) come into existence and endure.

The fourth argument for the existence of God is the moral. It runs like this. Even the most secular people act as if moral values have a real existence; love is good, hatred is wrong; freedom is good, slavery is wrong; truth is good, lies are wrong. If moral values are objective, they surely point to a moral lawgiver (and judge). This was the argument of Kant. It is very convincing to many today, for few serious unbelievers are willing to say that the great moral values are no more than personal preferences; when you say "murder is evil" you mean more than "I don't like murder."

The Christian community evaluates these four arguments in different ways. It is not enough either to accept or reject them. A more specific evaluation is needed.

First, a distinction should be made between the question Is it true? and the question Does it help? An argument which is not true, should not be used. But even if an argument is true, it may not be helpful to people today. In our judgment, even if the ontological argument were true as an argument, it does not help most people to believe; it makes them feel as if they have been tricked. This is because people today do not rely upon rationality as much as medieval thinkers did; they are more empirical—they want evidence as well as reason.

Here are five more specific evaluations of the arguments. First, they may be held to provide evidence in support of God's existence. Thus, for example, human moral experiences may increase the probability that God exists, and the moral argument shows that.

Second, the arguments may be clues or hints of the reality of God. They do not argue; they suggest. Many people today, who resist the argumentative forms, are open to this more elusive form. Though it may seem a weaker form, for some people it actually is stronger, more convincing.

Third, the arguments may provide a jumping-off place from which a person can leap to a new insight; they may encourage an "aha!" experience, in which one suddenly sees: "Of course, there's a God! I should have seen it all along!" This is the position of philosopher H. D. Lewis.

Fourth, the arguments may be felt, by Christians, not to hold up. For example, John Hick argues that they hold only if a person believes the world makes sense—but one can always deny that the world makes sense. Thus the cosmological argument says that since the world exists, either there is a creator or the world makes no sense—but the atheist would still choose the latter option. If this position is held, one might say of the cosmological argument, for example, that it demonstrates that the world makes a certain kind of sense if there is a God and that it doesn't make that kind of sense if there is no God. This modest view is helpful to some people.

Fifth, some Christians deny that the arguments are proper at all. Theologian Gustaf Aulen says that any god who can be proved is not the God and Father of Jesus Christ. The arguments are, therefore, about idols.

For reasons given above, we do not accept Aulen's conclusion. But it does contain a kernel of truth. The God of the arguments is self-existent (the ontological argument), Creator (the cosmological), Designer (the teleological), Law-giver (the moral). But God is much more than this—he is also the Savior, the Spirit, the Lord, the Holy One. No philosophical argument has ever been devised which attempts to say this; this is learned only through God's self-revelation, especially in Jesus Christ.

PROMISE. A declaration that one will do a certain thing in the future.

Not all religions are concerned about history, time, and the future; some are concerned about timelessness and about rising above history. Stoicism taught that one should be indifferent toward the future.

The Jewish religion was very concerned about the future. God made promises to the patriarch Abraham and later to the people of Israel. Their attention was turned toward the future; they learned to expect, to anticipate, and to hope for the fulfillment of these promises in the future.

The early Christians saw in Jesus the fulfillment of the Old Testament promises. God had promised to bless the nation through Abraham's seed; this promise was fulfilled through Jesus. God had promised to create a people for himself; this promise was fulfilled through Jesus. God had promised a new age and a new covenant with people, written on their hearts rather than on stones; this promise was fulfilled in Jesus. God had promised that David's descendants would rule forever; this promise was fulfilled in Jesus. The promise-fulfillment theme runs through the New Testament; it is especially clear in Matthew's Gospel.

It was inevitable that the early church understood Jesus in terms of the Old Testament; they were Jewish people, and no other religious understanding of Jesus was conceivable to them. Had Jesus not somehow fulfilled the promises of the Old Testament, he would have been religiously unimportant to these people. Yet, he did not fulfill things exactly as they expected them. For example, he was the anointed, the Christ—but not a military or apocalyptic Christ. Along with fulfillment, therefore, Jesus brought innovation. The new wine burst some of the old wineskins. He was more than they had hoped for; he was superior to even their greatest hopes.

Sometimes the New Testament seems to portray Jesus as fulfilling Old Testament hopes with great exactness and precision, as when Matthew tells of the flight into Egypt (2:13-15; Hos. 11:1). This kind of precision troubles some modern readers, who ask historically-minded questions such as, Was Hosea thinking of Jesus in this prophecy? The answer, in this case, is that Hosea was talking about Israel, as he said, not about Jesus. Taken as precise prophecy, this is problematic; but the biblical writers were men of broader than historical sympathies. In this case, what was Matthew's point? God saved Israel from Egypt; God is now doing his saving work through Jesus Christ; and Jesus, like Israel, is led back from Egypt by God.

Other passages make clear in other ways the flexibility which the early Christians felt toward the Old Testament text. For example, in his Pentecost sermon, Peter said that what was then happening (speaking in tongues, tongues of fire, sound of rushing wind) was a fulfillment of a prophecy in Joel (Acts 2:14-21; Joel 2:28-30). He quoted as fulfilled a saying about the sun being turned to darkness and the moon to blood. These words were fulfilled figuratively, not literally. On the other hand, the words about God pouring out his Spirit on all kinds of people (not just on leaders, as he had done in the Old Testament), were fulfilled literally, for all the Christians then received the gift of the Spirit.

In summary, the early church saw in Jesus Christ the fulfillment of the promises given by God to the nation Israel.

Further, in Jesus Christ, God gave new promises. The most important of these was the promise of eternal life. This was given in the words of Jesus, but especially in his resurrection. As Paul put it, Christ is the firstfruits of resurrection (1 Cor. 15:20), that is, the first to be raised and the promise that others shall also be raised. This promise remains to be fulfilled in the future. Thus Christians today are to live with the faith that God will fulfill all the promises he made in Jesus Christ; that is the Christian hope.

PROVIDENCE. God's ability to foresee the future and to make provisions for it.

Christians speak of the providence of God to describe his continuing interest and care for all creation, particularly his loving care for his own people.

There are four basic conclusions which one may draw concerning the providence of God. First, nothing happens in our world without God's permission. The fact that the world itself continues to exist is a result of the providence of God. Second, not everything that happens is in accordance with God's will. The sin of people and the pollution of our atmosphere are indications of this truth. Determinism which teaches that all actions are predetermined by outside forces does not explain human behavior. People are influenced but not completely determined by factors, such as their genetic makeup, their families, and their societies. Third, God can take any circumstance and bring something good out of it (Rom. 8:28). Fourth, we have the responsibility for seeking to know the mind of God and for conforming to it. God will ultimately bring his will to pass, but he wishes his will to be done by people on earth, even as it is in heaven. The mind of God and his will for our lives were ultimately revealed in the life and teachings of Jesus.

R

REASON. The human ability to think rationally.

In the creation story, God created man and woman and was pleased with what had been created. Since they had rational faculties, it is assumed that their reason was also deemed to be good.

Like all other aspects of human life, reason has been adversely affected by sin. In the Old Testament, this impairment of reasoning ability is made clear in that true wisdom is not a natural endowment but is a special gift from God (Dan. 2:20-21).

Jesus emphasized in his teachings the distinction between the wisdom of God and the wisdom of humanity (Matt. 11:25-26). However, he did not encourage his followers to cease thinking. On the contrary, he urged them to think carefully and calculate wisely (Matt. 10:16). Further, he promised to give his followers wisdom in times of tribulation (Luke 21:15).

Reason is sometimes contrasted with faith, as if one must choose between them. This is a misunderstanding of the nature of rationality. Reason can as easily lead one toward faith as away from it. Reason is a tool which may be used in grasping the truth of God, or it may be a defense mechanism to prevent God's truth from penetrating to the depths of one's being.

RECONCILIATION. The changed relationship between God and a person that is brought about by Christ's death and resurrection.

A number of metaphors in the New Testament describe what Christ accomplished by means of his death and resurrection, including justification, new birth, salvation, redemption, and others. Reconciliation is one of these metaphors and a favorite of Paul's. He used it in four of his letters (Rom. 5:10; 2 Cor. 5:18; Eph. 2:16; Col. 1:20).

Paul understood reconciliation as a rapprochement between God and humanity. They are brought together not as a mutual act, but as a unilateral act by God in Christ. People are estranged from God by sin and, therefore, are unwilling and unable to restore fellowship with God. God acts in Christ to break down the barriers that prevent people from having fellowship with God. This act of God is not coercive. A person is still free to reject God's love and friendship, but he now has the opportunity through Christ to be restored to his intended relationship with God (2 Cor. 5:18-20).

This reconciliation between God and humanity is also intended to affect the relationships between human beings. Just as we are estranged from God, we also are estranged from ourselves and our fellowmen. Because we are loved and accepted by God, we are now free to love others (1 John 4:7-12). God's intention is that this reconciliation, brought about by Christ, should affect the entire universe. "For God was pleased to have all his fullness dwell in him, and through him to reconcile to himself all things, whether things on earth or things in heaven" (Col. 1:19-20, authors' translation).

REDEMPTION. Liberation from sin and death.

Redemption is one of several New Testament descriptions of the salvation which Christ provided. When the human problem is understood as transgression of the law, salvation is described as justification. When the human problem is understood as spiritual deadness, salvation is described as regeneration. When the human problem is understood as slavery to sin and death, salvation is described as redemption, that is, as liberation. The greatest redemption of the Old Testament was God's liberation of Israel from slavery in Egypt.

Redemption is accomplished by the payment of a price; in Greek the words *redeem* and *ransom* are etymologically related. A slave or soldier captured in battle could be redeemed by a ransom. Jesus spoke of giving his life as a ransom (Mark 10:45), and Paul referred to Christians having been "bought with a price" (1 Cor. 6:20). The image is a vivid and powerful one, and all Christians have an inner appreciation for it. They are very conscious that their new life is a gift which was freely given to them but which was infinitely costly to God.

Sometimes the question is asked, To whom did Christ pay the ransom? The principal answers are, either to God, or to the devil. The Bible does not answer the question, for the very good reason that it is not an appropriate question. The image of a price is to be understood in a flexible way, not in a rigid way. We today use the image freely at times. Thus it may be said, "She paid a great price to educate her children," or "He paid a great price to be a missionary." The meaning is quite clear, and it is not necessary to ask to whom these prices were paid.

Redemption is liberation from sin and death—but liberation to what? The best answer is, to a new relationship with God, and therefore, to forgiveness, life, peace, joy. *Redemption* and *forgiveness* are more or less synonymous terms in Ephesians 1:7 (see also Col. 1:14), which speaks of Christ "in whom we have redemption through his blood, the forgiveness of sins" (KJV). This means that Christ died to liberate people from slavery to sin and death—in other words, to provide forgiveness and a new relation with God.

Christ performed his great liberating work in the past, in the first century. That redemption is applied to people in the present as they accept Christ and are liberated by him. There also is a sense in which redemption will not be consummated until the future: we "wait for adoption as sons, the redemption of our bodies" (Rom. 8:23, authors' translation). There is nothing incomplete about what Christ achieved, but there is in the future a final and ultimate redemption in which God's people will be completely set free from all evil.

RELIGION. Belief in an ultimate reality or realities, together with an effort to relate properly to ultimate reality, usually including worship.

The biblical writers had no interest in religion, in the sense of common ground between Judaism (or Christianity) and the religions of neighbors such as Philistines or Romans. They were intent upon the differences, not the commonalities. The general concept of religion as a grouping together of the ultimate beliefs and practices of all the peoples of the world is a postbiblical one.

Religion is a universal phenomenon. No society or culture is known to have existed without religion. The fact of the universality of religion has been one of the factors offered by apologists to secular people as evidence in support of a transcendent reality. The argument is simply that a phenomenon so universal must have some basis in reality.

Religions vary enormously. Some are made up principally of moral and practical teachings (Confucianism). Others are polytheistic (Hinduism). Three are monotheistic (Judaism, Christianity, and Islam). Many ancient religions ceased to be practiced long ago. Some people distinguished between primitive and advanced religions, though this distinction is sometimes difficult to sustain. Some religions are local, such as Shinto in Japan. The largest of the world religions are Christianity, Islam, Hinduism, and Buddhism. Some scholars regard Marxism as a religion, though it is secular.

Scholars are divided on whether there is a fundamental human capacity or need, shared by all people, which can account for the universality of religion. Since most people in the past and present have participated in religion, the capacity for it seems to be universal. But is this capacity a uniquely religious factor, or is it rather that human beings follow traditions and religion happens to be traditional? Augustine expressed his conviction about a religious capacity when he wrote in his *Confessions:* "Lord, you have made us for yourself, and our hearts are restless until they find their rest in you." The most popular recent suggestion about a fundamental religious capacity is that of Rudolf Otto. He spoke of a *mysterium tremendum et fascinans*, that is, a profound mystery which repels us (frightens us) and yet also attracts us.

To that description must be added the qualifier: no one is religious simply because of his or her beliefs. Religion does not begin until a person acts upon those belief and attempts to become properly related to ultimate reality (God). The actions may be moral, cultic, or involve mystical experiences; they may be social or private; they may be traditional or innovative; they usually include worship. What is essential is that belief does not become religious until it leads one to act in a way which is appropriate to that belief.

Some theologians have argued that Christianity is not a religion. What they mean is this. In religions, people seek to discover God; in Christianity, God has revealed himself. In religions, people seek to please God; in Christianity, God graciously accepts people. This distinction is a useful one; there is a real difference between people moving toward God by works and God coming to people by grace. However, some of the other religions insist that they too believe in a God of grace and love. Further, the distinction between Christianity and the other religions can be made without denying that Christianity is a religion; one may say simply that Christianity is a religion of divine grace not of human effort. This ought to be done since, as a matter of fact, Christianity is one of the religions of humanity. In fact, it is the largest of all the world religions, the dominant religion of Europe and the Americas, and the fastest growing religion in Africa. It is confusing to outsiders to deny that Christianity is a religion.

REPENTANCE. Turning from sin to God.

The New Testament word for repentance means to change one's mind, and a Pauline phrase could serve as a definition for the term: "You turned to God from idols, to serve a living and true God" (1 Thess. 1:9).

Repentance is the initial response which a person must make in order to become a Christian. It also is a response which

Christians must make repeatedly throughout their pilgrimage, for even the best Christian does not live life perfectly for God. Repentance is thus a metaphor for faith; faith is personal trust in God, and repentance pictures that trust as turning to God.

Repentance may be distinguished from three other responses to God which are clearly related to and often accompany repentance. They are sorrow for sin (penitence or contrition), admission of sin (confession), and resolve to give up sin. These are appropriate responses for a repentant person to make. However, taken together or singly, they do not comprise repentance. These terms speak of a response made to sin; repentance speaks of a response made specifically to God. It is not enough to turn away from sin; one must also turn to God.

In fact, surprising as it may seem, it is possible to become so preoccupied with one's sin—regretting it, renouncing it—that one's attention is thereby directed away from God and from the gospel. The preacher of the gospel must direct the attention of the listener away from himself—including his sin—toward Christ. In Acts the apostles in their sermons never attempted to convince people of sin; they always attempted to convince them of what God had achieved in Christ.

RESURRECTION. God's restoration to life of Christ and Christians after their deaths.

The idea of resurrection was widespread among Jews by the time of Jesus' ministry. Though the details were not worked out, many Jews believed that God would resurrect the righteous as a reward for faithfulness.

Jesus transformed this Jewish understanding through his own resurrection. The New Testament teaches that Jesus was resurrected through the power of God (Acts 2:24). The witness to his resurrection includes the empty tomb (John 20) and his appearances to his disciples after his death (1 Cor. 15). The growth of the church and the willingness of Christ's disciples to die in his service are eloquent testimonies to their confidence in his resurrection.

Because the resurrection of Jesus was unique, it is not

surprising to find anomalies in the descriptions left us by those who saw him. He had a body, but he was capable of appearing or disappearing at will (John 20:26-28). He was recognizable, yet somehow different so that he was not immediately recognized even by some of his followers (Luke 24). The Gospels and Acts affirm that Jesus' appearances climaxed in his ascension to be with the Father (Luke 24:51; Acts 1:9).

The resurrection of Jesus was understood by the first-century Christians as a sign. It authenticated the things that Jesus taught and the claims he made about himself. His resurrection was seen as the inauguration of a new era in the relations between God and people.

The New Testament teaches that Jesus' resurrection is to be shared by all believers. Jesus promised to come back to get his followers (John 14:3). This resurrection of believers is described in some detail by the apostle Paul. His confidence in the resurrection of believers was based upon the resurrection of Jesus. If Jesus' resurrection were not real, then we have no hope of being resurrected ourselves (1 Cor. 15:17). Jesus spoke of the resurrection of nonbelievers. These shall be raised for judgment (John 5:28-29).

Though the details of what believers' resurrection will be like are sketchy, some clues are given in the New Testament. We will have bodies after our resurrection. But like Jesus, our resurrected bodies will be spiritual and, therefore, different from our physical bodies (1 Cor. 15:44). John specifically taught that we shall be like Christ (1 John 3:2).

The resurrection is the heart of the Christian faith. Without it Jesus' death on the cross is just another martyr's death. If he were not raised from the dead, then we could have no confidence in his authority to interpret God to us and we could not accept his claim to be God's only Son. Because he is resurrected, believers can face their own lives and deaths with confidence (Col. 3:1-4).

REVELATION. God's self-disclosure to humanity.

The meaning of the New Testament term is uncovering. The cluster of ideas related to revelation includes: first, God is somehow hidden or mysterious; second, God wants people to know him; third, people cannot discover God by their own efforts; fourth, God acts to show himself to people.

Many of the church's debates about revelation have been no more than verbal problems, arguments about how the term *revelation* should be used. These debates are futile. The term is used in a very restricted sense in the Bible. Its use has been enlarged in the church's theology. Whether it should, for example, be used of God's acts in history or also of the interpretation of these acts is an arbitrary matter. Again, whether the personal encounter with God should be called revelation, or whether the knowledge about God which the person has, should be called revelation is a matter of little importance. These are debates about how a word is to be used. The real questions are: does God act in history to reveal himself? Does God provide an authorized interpretation of his acts in history? Does God thereby provide persons with an understanding of themselves? Does God do this in order that the person may enter into a relationship of love and trust toward God? The correct answer to all these questions is yes. It does not matter whether one uses the world *revelation* of these or not. For convenience's sake, the word will be used of all four in this essay.

In the past, theologians distinguished between a knowledge of God which could be obtained by reason alone and without benefit of revelation (the knowledge, for example, that God exists) and a knowledge of God which could only come by revelation (for example, the knowledge of the Trinity). These were called natural truths and revealed truths, respectively. The distinction is a misleading one, for it has as a hidden assumption the untrue idea that God is not active in all the universe. But God is active throughout the universe. Therefore, whenever any person arrives at any true understanding of God, however partial or distorted, the grain of truth has been made possible by God himself. All knowledge of God is given by revelation; people cannot discover God alone for the very good reason that they are never alone; God is always present.

A more judicious distinction is between the knowledge of himself which God provides in creation and the knowledge of himself which he provides in history, specifically the history of the Jewish people which received its fulfillment in Jesus Christ. These are known as general and special revelation.

Concerning general revelation, four questions need to be reviewed. First, has God given and can a person receive a general revelation? Second, if God has given a general revelation, how is it mediated? Third, what may be known about God through general revelation alone? Fourth, what is the relation of general revelation to special revelation? Only a brief response can be given to each of these questions.

The Bible suggests that nature somehow reveals God. In a sermon at Lystra, Paul spoke of the awesomeness, order, and bounty of nature. He said that God "did not leave himself without witness" among the Gentiles because nature testified to the reality of God (Acts 14:8-18). Paul informed the Roman church that no one can be exonerated of sin since God has shown people what may be known of himself ever since the creation of the world, even his power and deity (Rom. 1:19-20). In addition to these and similar biblical passages, it has often been observed that, in fact, a knowledge of God is widespread among people, though it is a restricted and distorted knowledge. It, therefore, may be concluded that God gives a general knowledge of himself, through the world he created, in something like the way in which a novel may reveal something of its author.

But can people receive this knowledge, or has sin so distorted their minds that though God sends his message people do not receive it? There is no doubt that sin has distorted and restricted people's reception of God's revelation. However, some of the message gets through. The texts quoted earlier affirm this, and an examination of the situation in people's lives confirms it.

How, then, is the general knowledge of God mediated? The first observation to be made is this: as the transcendent Lord, God may use any medium he chooses to convey his self-revelation. No one is in a position to say that God cannot have spoken through a particular medium. This is true of general and of special revelation.

Beyond this, one must observe that God may well be using far more media than any one of us recognizes. A few examples must do. Through nature, God reveals that he is Creator. Through moral law, God reveals his moral concerns. Through a haunting experience of futility and pointlessness, God reveals that there is a transcendent meaning of life. Through family relations, God reveals that he loves and cares for persons as a good parent does his children. The list could be extended.

Third, it is not possible to say exactly what may be known about God through general revelation. Presumably one may know that God exists; perhaps that God is one; perhaps that he is holy; perhaps that he is love; surely not that he is Father, Son, and Holy Spirit. In other words, when one moves on to the distinctly Christian understanding of God, by definition one has moved from general to special revelation, that is, from the revelation given in nature to that given in the history of Jesus. Thus, one must hear and accept a special revelation if one is to become a Christian.

Finally, the usual assumption is that the relation of general to special revelation is that general revelation prepares people's minds to receive the special revelation. Often this is true, but there is more to be said. In our time, the secular challenge to religious belief is often effective against the general revelation of God. At times, it is only when one receives the special revelation given in Jesus that one can accept the very existence of God. To put it the other way around, belief in Jesus is not always an additional belief to belief in God but in fact may be a prerequisite to it. One may argue that this is not logical, but people are not always logical. And, in any case, it has a logic of its own.

Also, general revelation may have a role to play in the life of the person who has accepted the special revelation. It may continue to inform a Christian about God, particularly about the universality of God's concerns, purposes, and activities.

Perhaps these basic remarks demonstrate that general

revelation is a complex and controversial subject. In any case, special revelation is even more complex and controversial. It will be discussed under three headings: revelation as history, revelation as language, and revelation as encounter. These three form a chronological sequence and a logical one.

The Bible is, among other things, a record of a number of mighty acts which God performed in the history of the Jewish people. Representative of these acts are the call of Abraham, the deliverance at the Exodus and formation of the people into a nation, the gift of the land, the leadership of David, the deliverance from captivity in Babylon, and especially the life, work, death, and resurrection of Jesus Christ, followed by the gift of the Spirit and the formation of the church.

By these acts, God showed his people what he was like. He revealed his purposes and his character. He is, for example, a God of power, wisdom, love, and patience. His purpose is to have a people for his own, to love them and be loved in return, and so on. The acts of God reveal God to humanity and much more about God than was revealed in the general revelation through nature.

Not all God's acts in history are of the same importance. The writer of Hebrews expressed in classic form the priority of the revelation given in Jesus: "In many and various ways God spoke of old to our fathers by the prophets: but in these last days he has spoken to us by a Son" (Heb. 1:1; compare also Jesus' parable of the wicked husbandman, Mark 12:1-7). The superiority of this revelation of God given in Christ may be explained in various ways, for example, in the poignancy of his parables. But the final explanation is that given by John: "And the Word became flesh and dwelt among us, full of grace and truth: we have beheld his glory, glory as of the only Son from the Father. No one has ever seen God; the only Son who is in the bosom of the Father, he has made him known" (John 1:14,18). The ultimacy and finality of the revelation given in Jesus reside in the fact that Jesus of Nazareth was the incarnation of God's Son. Therefore, every act of Jesus was an act of God; every attitude of Jesus, an attitude of God; every word of Jesus, a word of God; Jesus was the very image of

God, the fullest word of God ever spoken or ever to be spoken, for he was Emmanuel, God with us.

Special revelation thus begins with God acting in history, supremely in his Son, Jesus. This fact brings us face-to-face with one of the most perplexing problems in Christian theology, the scandal of particularity. Why the Jews? Why this particular history? Why Jesus Christ? Why must our knowledge of the eternal, transcendent God rest on the narrow foundation of this story rather than any other? Though no answer is entirely satisfactory to all persons, at least part of the truth is that if God were to act in a saving way on people's behalf, he had do so in the only arena in which actions are meaningful to human beings, the arena of history. Particularity was inevitable, therefore, if God were to act. And if he did not act, there would have been no saving revelation.

Historical events are never transmitted as raw data. They are interpreted. All historical accounts involve some interpretation if it be no more than the judgment that the event reported was worthy of being reported. The revelatory acts of God certainly were not reported neutrally. They were recorded and transmitted with their interpretations intact. To the event—"Christ died"—the prophets and apostles added their interpretation—"for our sins, according to the scriptures" (1 Cor. 15:3). The prophetic and apostolic witness and interpretation had to be both authoritative and indispensable if the divine acts were to have continuing revelatory value for God's people. The Bible may be understood as containing the witness to God's mightly acts and the authoritative interpretation of those acts; of course, it also contains other material, such as proverbs and songs. But given the importance of the divine acts to the life of Israel and the church, it is not too farfetched to see even these other types of literature as authorized responses to God's acts.

Special revelation, thus, begins with historical acts and continues in a book of literature, the Bible, which contains the witness to and authorized interpretation of those acts. In that sense, the Bible, like the acts themselves, is divine revelation; it too is the very Word of the Lord.

Since the Bible is made up of words and sentences, the tendency of many theologies has been to see its sentences as revelatory independently of the acts of God to which it bears witness. This is unwarranted, for the Bible was not intended by God to function independently of the mighty acts, but to bear witness to the mighty acts of God. The most pernicious effort at making the text independent of the acts is to treat the sentences as propositions which affirm timeless truths and timeless abstractions divorced from history. But the language of the Bible is in a vital sense timely, and its timeless message—a message to people of all times—is timeless precisely because it is so timely, so attached to its own time and place. Some of the biblical affirmations may be treated as propositions in the logical sense with a minimum of misunderstanding; perhaps "God is love" would be a good example (1 John 4:8). Far more of the biblical affirmations require that their attachment to the acts of God be made explicit if their truth is to be clear; for example, the affirmation that "God is love" is made much fuller by John's other statement, "God so loved the world, that he gave his only begotten Son" (John 3:16, KJV). The meaning of love is thus made more explicit: it is not sentimentalism or passion; it is a saving act.

This may be put another way. The truth of the Bible is not exhausted by seeing it as a collection of propositions. It witnesses to and interprets historical acts. It expresses the truth of God not only by propositions but also by a vast cascade of images, metaphors, allusions, symbols, and other literary forms. Thus, God is a rock, a Father, a shepherd, an eagle, a Savior, a Spirit, a king, a warrior, a judge, and so on. There is truth here; profound truth-claims are being made, but the forms of the affirmation are more varied and elusive than the term *proposition* suggests.

God acts in history, especially in Christ; the Bible contains the authorized witness and interpretation of his acts. But the Bible is not the only body of words which attempts to bear witness to God's acts. So do countless sermons, books, hymns, and personal conversations which have been produced since the

Bible was written. In a sense, these words too are revelatory; that is, God uses the words of people to reveal himself to their listeners and readers. This is the word of God as preached by the people of God.

Most Christians agree about this. But it creates a problem. If the Bible is a revelation, in what sense is the Bible unique? The answer is that the Bible is the authorized witness and the authorized interpretation. It is the verbal norm. Against it, all other verbal witness should be measured. Its authority is often expressed this way: the Bible is God's revelation, and God uses the witness of other people to reveal himself. However it is expressed, the Bible's unique place in the pattern of revelation should be made clear.

At this point, one's understanding of the purpose of revelation becomes important. Is God's purpose just to provide people with understanding? If so, then the views developed thus far would be complete: through nature God reveals his existence; through acts in history he enlarges that revelation; through the Bible (and preaching) that revelation becomes written. What is missing? It is the recognition that God's concern is not only that people understand about him but also that they respond to God in trust and love. Our understanding of God is one ingredient to contribute to the goal of our encounter with God. God gives us truth about himself so that he may give us the even more precious gift of himself. Knowledge alone is not the fulfillment of God's purpose. Conversely, encounter alone (without knowledge) is a meaningless idea and is not a response of the whole person to God (since it would not include a response of the understanding). "He that cometh to God must believe that he is" (Heb. 11:16, KJV).

In other words, the divine revelation is given so that persons may know about God and then may know God in a personal relationship.

This pattern of revelation seems to touch the major concerns of modern theology about revelation, though in a very brief way. Two things remain to be said about God's self-disclosure.

First, it is a matter of sheer grace. We do not deserve God's revelation of himself and should never presume upon it. Only because God is kind and loving did he sprinkle nature with traces of his power. Only because he is gracious did he call a people who were no people to be his own. Only because he is the God of infinite love did he send his Son to be the Savior of the world. Only because of his concern for humanity did he inspire the writing of a Bible to mediate his message. And only because of his compassion does he meet people who receive his revelation with gifts of forgiveness, peace, and life.

Finally, Christian theology requires some affirmation of a revelation, whether construed as above or in some other way. It is no good trying to construct a theology that is really Christian unless one accepts that somehow God has disclosed himself to people. This fact, which ought to be obvious, is sometimes overlooked by theologians seeking to do their work in our secular milieu.

REVIVAL. A renewal of religious commitment within the church.

Though not a biblical word, the idea of *revival* is found in the Bible. Paul encouraged repentance among the Christians at Corinth and rejoiced when they turned from their sin (2 Cor. 7:9-10).

Revivalism—the practice of having a series of days set aside for intense praying and preaching—was first practiced by the Methodists in the eighteenth century. It has remained a feature of Evangelical worship, though the popularity of extended revival meetings may be waning.

Sometimes the word is used to describe a national spiritual awakening, such as was experienced in the Great Awakening in America in the early nineteenth century. This call for a renewed religious commitment in the nation is often justified by the appeal to 2 Chronicles 7:14. While this text does not refer to the modern international situation, it is true that God responds to the prayers of his people. And when God's people pray, the likely result is revival.

RIGHTEOUSNESS. God's self-consistency.

The Jews were the first people to assert that God is neither arbitrary nor capricious. They described him as righteous. From this it followed that God requires the righteous conduct of people. This entails conformity to God's moral standards: we must love God and love our neighbor (Matt. 22:37-40).

Since we do not obey this law, we deserve God's judgment and condemnation. However, because God loves us, he sent his Son to take our place in judgment. Through our faith in Jesus as Lord and Savior, his righteousness is imparted by God to us (Phil. 3:9; Rom. 5:1-2). The coming of the Holy Spirit into the lives of Christians empowers them to grow into conformity with God's righteousness.

Thus for the Christian righteousness is four things: one of God's perfections, a requirement from God that we conform to his righteous character, a gift of God through faith in Jesus Christ, and the new life in Christ that results.

S

SABBATH. The day reserved for worshiping God and for rest.

The word *sabbath* comes from a word meaning to desist or stop. The idea of a sabbath, or rest day, may be traced to the Genesis account of creation. On the seventh day God rested. Observance of the seventh day and of circumcision became the identifying characteristics of the Jewish people (Ex. 31:12). Sabbath observance was understood to be a mandate from God (Ex. 20:8-11). To profane the sabbath was to disobey God, so the Jewish people carefully circumscribed the sabbath with rituals and laws which prevented one from commiting this sin.

Jesus was regarded as presumptuous by some of his contemporaries because he did not observe the petty rules which were observed by the religious leaders of his day. His understanding was a clear return to the sabbath's original purpose—a rest for people. Jesus' definitive statement was, "The sabbath was made for man, not man for the sabbath" (Mark 2:27).

What was more shocking to his contemporaries was his claim to be "Lord even of the sabbath" (Mark 2:28). Jesus demonstrated this by repeatedly performing healing miracles on the sabbath (Mark 1:21 *ff.*).

For Christians the sabbath, or holy day, has been changed from Saturday, the seventh day, to Sunday, the first day of the week. The change came about as a result of Jesus' resurrection on Sunday (John 20:1) and the coming of the Holy Spirit on that day (Acts 2:1). It became the custom of the early church to celebrate that day, and increasingly the church moved away from the observance of the Jewish sabbath to the distinctively Christian sabbath day—Sunday.

SACRIFICE. An offering given to God.

Like religion itself, sacrifice seems to have been universal in the ancient world. The story of Cain and Abel (Gen. 4:1-16) shows that the Jews understood sacrifice to have originated with the earliest people.

The Hebrew people began to practice sacrifices in Egypt (the Passover) and continued to do so in the Land of Canaan. After King Josiah's reform, no sacrifices could be offered in groves and high places; all were transferred to the Temple. Several prophets protested against abuses of the sacrificial system. Hosea is representative: "For I desire steadfast love and not sacrifice, the knowledge of God, rather than burnt offerings" (6:6).

Sacrifice was an integral part of Israel's worship. Various sacrifices were understood in various ways. Some were simply expressions of thanksgiving for God's blessings, particularly in harvest. Others were understood as providing and maintaining communion with God, as when the flesh of an animal was partly burned (offered to God) and partly eaten by the worshipers. Some (sin offerings) were designed to provide forgiveness for sins. Scholars are divided on the question of how the sacrifices were understood to provide forgiveness. Most agree that God's favor was not bought by the sin offerings. Some believe that the sin offerings were propitiatory: they deflected the wrath of God away from sinners. Others deny this and say that the sin offerings were expiatory: they were the means provided by God for cleansing sinners and making them acceptable to God. Another alternative, not so widely held as these two, is that neither of these rationales dominated. What dominated was a presupposition, so obvious that it needed no defense, that sacrificial blood takes away sin. If this is true, then no explanation would ever have been needed to explain how sacrifice worked, and expiatory and propitiatory language might have been used alternatively with no sense of tension.

The early Christians became the first religious group in the Roman Empire not to practice sacrifice, followed by the Jews when the Temple was destroyed in AD 70. As a result of the dominance of Christianity and Judaism, animal sacrifices are not part of Western culture today. Their absence should not conceal from us the eccentricity of the Christians who first gave up sacrifice. What happened to cause the church to worship without animal sacrifices?

Jesus himself seems to have tolerated the sacrificial system, but his sympathies were on the side of the prophets who proclaimed that forgiveness is for all who repent and that God wants people to be righteous more than he wants them to offer sacrifices. Jesus quoted the passage from Hosea given previously (see Matt. 9:13). He also spoke of the destruction of the Temple, which would bring about the end of the Jewish sacrifice.

On the other hand, he used sacrificial language of his own work (as, Mark 10:45). The background for this may have been the Suffering Servant of whom Isaiah spoke (Isa. 53). In particular, Jesus referred to the blood which he would shed at his crucifixion as providing forgiveness and as making a new covenant between God and people (Matt. 26:26-29). This is explicitly sacrificial language, the language of sin offerings, which is all the more astonishing because the Hebrews had totally rejected human sacrifice as practiced by some of their neighbors in Canaan.

The early Christian proclamation included "that Christ died for our sins" (1 Cor. 15:3), and the idea of Christ's death as sacrificial occurs frequently throughout the New Testament. No writer developed this theme in more detail than the author of Hebrews. He argued, among other things, that Christ's sacrifice was superior to those of the Jewish system because it was once for all, it was voluntary, it was morally as well as ritually pure, and Christ was both the High Priest (offerer) and the victim (offering). The Old Testament had taught that God had graciously provided the sacrificial system; the writer of Hebrews believed that God had provided the sacrifice as well. This was part of his plea to Jewish Christians not to return to the sacrificial system which Christ had rendered obsolete. It was this argument which was the rationale which led the Christian community to become the first religion in the Roman world to function without animal sacrifices.

The church did maintain a spiritualized understanding of sacrifice: Christians were to commit their lives to Christ as living sacrifices, which was, after all, only reasonable worship for those for whom salvation had been provided by the sacrifice of Christ (Rom. 12:1-2). The church also continued to remember, and in some sense reenact and relive, the sacrifice of Christ, through the practice of the Lord's Supper which, therefore, was spoken of in sacrificial language.

SALVATION. God's gracious gift, through Jesus Christ, of deliverance from sin and forgiveness of sins, and of a new relationship to God.

The Old Testament background of the Christian doctrine of salvation is that God saved his people from Egyptian bondage and delivered them through the Exodus to become a nation and to have a land of their own. The Old Testament spoke of salvation also as God's deliverance of his people from their enemies, however these were perceived. For example, in Psalm 107, the redeemed are to be thankful for God's salvation and to confess it openly. God had delivered those who were lost in a desert (vv. 4-9), who were imprisoned (vv. 10-16), who were sick (vv. 17-22), and who were at sea during a storm (vv. 23-32). The Old Testament made it clear that people had a real need for salvation, that God is the Savior and that people must ask God to save them.

The New Testament develops its emphasis against this background. Human need for salvation is expressed as sickness, death, wrath, and sin. God has provided for our salvation by sending Jesus Christ. We must receive God's gracious provision by having faith in Jesus Christ. Paul was particularly careful to emphasize that salvation is given to the person who trusts Christ rather than to the one who keeps the law, thus making clear that God alone can save and also that he does so freely and graciously, never as a reward for merit. Salvation is thus a very personal matter, requiring the response of each individual. Yet it is also a social matter, for by definition the person who receives the gift of salvation becomes a part of the new community of faith.

The Greek word for *salvation* has as its root meaning health and wholeness. In Christian theology, it has lost this specific emphasis and has become an umbrella term, while other words such as *redemption, justification,* and *forgiveness* are used as more specific descriptions of what God provides in salvation. There is no special reason that this is so; it just happens to have developed in this way.

A contrast is sometimes made between Roman Catholic and Protestant understandings of salvation. It is said that the Catholic view sees sin as inner corruption; it sees human salvation as transformation from a bad to a good nature (deification; see 2 Pet. 1:3-7); and it sees the sacraments, especially the Eucharist, as the principal means for achieving this. Protestants, it is said, see sin as rebellion; they see salvation as reconciliation with God; and they see preaching as the principal means for achieving this. Whether these distinctions were ever so rigid and whether they continue to be appropriate after the Second Vatican Council are debatable matters. What is not debatable is that Catholics and Protestants agree that human beings are sinners in need of salvation, that they cannot save themselves, that only God can save them, that he has provided salvation in Jesus Christ, and that salvation is a free and gracious gift of God to people.

Protestant teachings about salvation have taken a distinctive direction in that they speak of salvation in three tenses. Christians can say that they were saved in the past, meaning that they were forgiven by God of their sins when they first trusted Jesus Christ to save them. They also can say that they are being saved in the present, meaning that God is continuing to work in their lives to make them into better persons. And they can say also that they shall be saved, meaning that in the future (after death) they shall be delivered finally from all their sins and made perfect in the presence of the eternal God. These three have traditionally been named justification (or regeneration), sanctification, and glorification, though the terms are somewhat arbitrary and it is the realities which matter, not the terms.

SANCTIFICATION. God's work of transforming a Christian into a good person.

Etymologically, the root meanings of the words *holy* and *sanctify* are the same: to set apart. The Jewish people regarded God as holy, as the utterly transcendent Lord. People and objects which were associated with God were thereby sanctified, or set apart. Thus, the Temple was holy, the law was holy, and the people themselves were holy. This respect for the unique holiness of God, together paradoxically with a recognition of the sacred quality of things on earth, is found in some forms in various religions.

In Christian theology, *holiness* and *sanctification* are moral terms. Sanctification is the work of God in the life of the Christian, transforming him into a good person. Some Christians have taught that it may be completed in this life, but most deny this. Some have also taught that a Christian may experience a second blessing by which the process of sanctification is instantly completed, but this view has not found universal approval. The consensus in the church today is that sanctification continues throughout a Christian's life and is completed only after death.

The work of transforming a Christian is done through various means, and probably no comprehensive, exact list of means of grace can be drawn up. The Bible, the church, Christian fellowship, Christian proclamation and teaching, and various forms of devotional life and nurture are means through which God's Spirit does his transforming work.

Sanctification is God's work, and it is a gift to Christians. Yet somehow the Christians cooperate in it, for Christians are to strive to resist temptation, to discipline themselves, to set their minds on noble qualities, and to serve others unselfishly. Yet when they have done their best, they realize that whatever is good in their lives is a gift from God. This is the paradox of grace. Perhaps the best metaphor for it is that of growth. Christians are urged to grow in grace and in the knowledge of Jesus Christ (2 Pet. 3:18); yet their growth is really a work of the Spirit who alone can produce in them fruits, such as love, joy, and peace (Gal. 5:22).

Sanctification must be guarded against two misunderstandings, the other-worldly and the legalistic. Other-worldy sanctification teaches that people are always seduced into sin by this world and urges Christians to withdraw from the affairs of the present life—such as marriage, family, politics, and business—and to enter into an isolated community of religion alone. Protestantism has rejected this monastic drift and has insisted that Christians can become just as sanctified in the world—where their influence is so desperately needed—as they can in a monastery. Jesus wanted his disciples to be in this world but not of it (John 17:15-19), as indeed he himself was. John the Baptist may have been an ascetic, but Jesus was not.

The legalistic misunderstanding of sanctification teaches that God's rules, which may almost be arbitrary, are to be kept whether or not one sees the point. But the demands of God are not arbitrary, and Christians very much need to see their point. Jesus taught explicitly that his disciples should serve him as friends rather than as slaves, in the sense that slaves may not see the point of their service but friends do (John 15:15). And he also made very explicit what the point of the law is: it is to love God and neighbor. Thus sanctification is God's work of transforming Christians into people who love God more and more and who love their neighbors more and more. Sanctification is thus not an unattractive and eccentric life to which the Christian is set apart but is precisely a life of wholeness, balance, simplicity, community, trust, and joy. The way of Christ is the way of love.

SECULARISM. The modern philosophy of life which carries on as if God did not exist.

Secularism is a term first used in the nineteenth century to describe the contemporary world view of many nontheistic people. Secularists do not believe in an afterlife. They are not necessarily amoral, but often wish to alleviate suffering. They frequently believe in progress, science, and personal fulfillment.

Some secularists are antireligious, but many simply do not take religious faith seriously. The Christian apologist must, therefore, seek to convince the former and engage the latter.

SECURITY OF THE BELIEVER. The guaranty that God will never forsake one of his children.

Salvation in the Old Testament originally meant providing for one's physical and material needs. Increasingly, this became expanded to include life after death. By the time of Jesus, there was an increasing interest in eternal salvation. The Christian gospel proclaimed that eternal life was to be found through a personal relationship with the risen Christ (Rom. 5:1-2).

This claim of eternal salvation raises a question concerning the once-for-all nature of the salvation experience. Is it possible for a Christian to lose his salvation? Some biblical passages have been interpreted to say that salvation may be forfeited. Galatians 5:4 speaks of those "fallen away from grace." Second Corinthians 6:1 warns against receiving God's grace in vain. Hebrews 6:6 refers to those "fall away" (KJV).

It is neither possible nor appropriate for us to put ourselves in God's place as judge of people, but it is possible to draw some conclusions about the security a believer may have in his salvation. It is true that some people who claim to be Christians later renounce their faith. Since we are not in a position to judge their spiritual condition, we can only accept at face value what they say about their relationship to God. If they say they are Christians, we believe them. If they say they aren't Christians, we believe them.

On the other hand, God has promised to be faithful to those who trust in Christ (1 Cor. 10:13). Since God has unconditionally promised to save those who trust in Christ, it would seem to make God duplicitous if he arbitrarily added additional criteria to the requirements for salvation. For example, if believers must promise to be faithful to certain actions for a lifetime, then we are reverting to Judaism by replacing God's grace with our works (Rom. 3:21-24). God may discipline, even punish, Christians who sin, but he will not forsake them (Rom. 6:23).

Closely related to the security of the believer is the assurance of salvation. While some Christians feel that it is presumptuous to say they are sure they have received eternal life, those who are in churches which have been touched by revivalism find that such confidence is natural, and they understand what Paul meant when he wrote: "I know whom I have believed, and I am sure that he is able to guard until that Day what has been entrusted to me" (2 Tim. 1:12). If it is God's purpose that his people feel fully confident of his love and grace, then it is not presumptuous of them to do so.

Many Christian leaders fear that, if people are completely confident of God's forgiveness, they may be led to immoral living. Two things may be said in response. First, true Christian living cannot be motivated by fear and uncertainty; no one will be a better Christian because he or she is unsure that he or she is a Christian. The heart of Christian living is love for God and people, and love is not compatible with fear. Fear that one is not a Christian, or that one may lose one's salvation, may motivate a person to go to church and to tithe and to renounce bad habits, but it will not motivate one to love. We do not love those who threaten us. Second, assurance of salvation and of eternal security often is the best motive for Christian living. If we are confident that God has fully accepted us and will never forsake us, we may be so moved by gratitude and trust that we love God obediently and serve others freely.

The position of some Calvinists was that believers could never lose their salvation, but that they could never be sure that they were truly saved. The position of early revivalists was that believers could be sure of their salvation, but they could forfeit it through disobedience or apostasy. The position of Baptists is that Christians can be sure of their salvation, and they can never lose it. This is the most positive possible stance for a Christian, and it results ideally in freedom from fear and freedom to serve God and others.

SIN. Personal and corporate rebellion against God.

Very few observers of the world today would describe the world as having no problems. Almost everyone agrees that humanity has serious problems. Some feel that the root problem is economic injustice; others say it is psychological maladjustment; others think it is political oppression; still others say it is dysfunction of educational systems. The Christian interpretation is that the root of all human problems is that people are out of touch with God; the biblical term for this is *sin*.

The origin of sin is traced to human disobedience of God in the creation story. The result of that disobedience was removal from God's presence (Gen. 3:23). The human situation is one of fallenness.

As a result of initial sin, people developed an inclination to sin again. That inclination has been called the sin nature. This inclination to sin influences people to continue to rebel against God (Rom. 5:12 *ff.*).

Because sin is so prevalent in all individual lives, the structures of society have become flawed. People have propagated their rebellion against God by structuring society in such a way that often no good choices are open to individuals. Instead, they must choose between two evils; they are trapped. Thus, we have personal sins and corporate sin.

The Bible records God's response to human sin and his efforts to save us from ourselves. The Bible is the story of salvation history. In the Old Testament, we read that God established a nation, gave that nation his laws, and acted to destroy sin through the pervasive influence of his people. Israel failed him, so he called out certain individuals to proclaim his message of love and forgiveness to those who would turn to him. These prophets went largely unheard.

God's final response to sin is detailed in the New Testament. He came into the world in the person of Jesus of Nazareth so as to identify with people. Jesus was tempted to sin like other people, but, unlike anyone else who had ever lived, he lived a sinless life. Having thus fulfilled God's original expectation for mankind, Jesus gave up his life as a sacrifice for the sins of others. His death and resurrection have inspired his followers to repent or turn from their sins and to place their trust in him as the Savior from their sins.

Christians must still continue to deal with sin in their lives and in the world. The difference is that they can be confident that God has a solution which works, namely, faith in Jesus Christ.

SOUL. A human being.

Neither the Hebrew word for soul *(nephesh)* nor the Greek word *(psyche)* is defined in the Bible, and the way in which they are used in the Bible is surprising to many Christians today. The Old Testament affirms, for example, that the Creator breathed into man's nostrils the breath of life and he *became* a living soul (Gen. 2:7), whereas a modern Christian might have expected the text to say that man's body *received* a living soul. Even more surprising, the same writer says that animals created by God are living souls (Gen. 1:24). Further, the New Testament speaks of it being praiseworthy for a person to lose his soul for the sake of the gospel (Mark 8:35-37), and it also speaks of God as being able to destroy both body and soul in hell (Matt. 10:28). Again, while the last text speaks of humans as body and soul, Paul could speak of a person as body, soul, and spirit (1 Thess. 5:23).

This usage is obviously very flexible, but that alone does not explain why it surprises the contemporary Christian. The explanation for the surprise is that in the years since the close of the New Testament, Christians have inherited usages for the word *soul* which are different from the biblical usages. These usages are inherited from Greek philosophy. Some of them are quite appropriate for Christians, whereas others actually go against biblical teaching. The simplest way to clarify this complex issue is to ask three questions which involve the term *soul* and see how they are to be answered.

The first question is: is the human soul a reality? The answer is both yes and no. Yes, to the naturalist. If a person denies all spiritual realities, including God, says that people are nothing more than bodies, and that death is the end of human existence, a Christian may quite properly affirm that people are more than animals; they are souls.

On the other hand, to a person who believes that people are made up of pure, eternal, spiritual souls and sinful, temporal, physical bodies and that for the soul to have eternal life in heaven it needs only to escape from the body at death, a Christian should say, no, we do not have souls in that sense. On almost every point a Christian must disagree. The Christian view is that a person is a unity of body and soul; God created both, body and soul, so both are good; however, both are affected by sin. The soul must receive eternal life as a gift from God, for it does not have it apart from God. And eternal life takes the form of the resurrection of the body as well as of the immortality of the soul.

The second question is: *is* a person a soul, or does a person *have* a soul? One may say that man has a soul, in that soul is not all that a man is, for he also is body. But on the whole, it is better to say that a man is a soul because he is a unity, and the soul (and mind, and will, and emotions, and so on) are analyses of the character and actions of the man rather than parts of a man.

The third question is: does God save souls or whole persons? Again, for the reasons given previously, both answers are possible. Because *soul* suggests to many people today the eternal aspect of a person, it is acceptable to say that God saves souls, meaning simply that the salvation which God gives is both for this present world and for eternity. But it is better to say that God saves the entire person, in that God is truly concerned about one's salvation now as well as in eternity.

Sometimes theological debates are about real differences, but sometimes they are only about words. The current debate about the soul is about words in that, when the issues are spelled out, Christians find that they are in agreement. The debate is only about how to use the word *soul*. In keeping with biblical usage, *soul* is defined herein as a human being.

SPIRITUAL GIFTS. Skills given by God to Christians for the benefit of the church.

Paul developed the idea of spiritual gifts, particularly in three epistles (1 Cor. 12—14; Rom. 12:1-8; Eph. 4:1-16). The Old Testament background for his teaching is the idea that the Spirit of God was given to selected individuals so that they might be equipped to serve God in special ways: to Joseph so he could interpret dreams (Gen. 41:38); to Bezalel so he could do carpentry (Ex. 31:2-3); to Othniel so he could be a judge (Judg. 3:9-10); to Gideon so he could lead in battle (Judg. 6:34); to Samson so he would be strong (Judg. 14:6, 19); and to others.

In the New Testament, Jesus received the Spirit in a special manner at his baptism (Matt. 3:13-17), and he was then directed by the Spirit first to be tempted (Matt. 4:1) and then to conduct his ministry (Luke 4:14). He promised to give the Spirit to his followers, a promise which was fulfilled at Pentecost (Acts 2:1-36). Just as the Spirit had equipped selected individuals in the Old Testament to serve God, so now he equipped all the members of the new community to serve God.

Paul believed that every Christian has a gift from God (1 Cor. 12:4-7). He did not attempt to draw up a comprehensive list of gifts; the lists in his letters represent his observations of what God had given the church, not a revelation of all possible gifts. Gifts which are highly valued in the church today, such as music, ability to work with children and youth, and counseling, are not mentioned by Paul.

By what criteria, then, could Paul recognize that the skills of members of the churches were gifts from God? There were two. First, no person who denies Christ and his gospel has received the Spirit or a gift of the Spirit (1 Cor. 12:1-3). Second, every gift which is from God may, and must, be used for the benefit of the church; these are spiritual gifts.

When this position is adopted, several troubling issues are resolved. First, are gifts received suddenly, or do they develop slowly? The answer is that it does not matter; a believer with skills which can help the church, whether these were received at once or slowly, has spiritual gifts. Can spiritual gifts be discovered, developed, and then used, just as non-Christians discover, develop, and use their natural talents? Again, the answer is yes; all that matters is that a person be a believer and that he or she have gifts which are usable for the benefit of the community of faith. These should be discovered, developed, and, of course, used.

Another question frequently asked is: are gifts separate from talents (Matt. 25:14-30) and from fruits of the Spirit (Gal. 5:22)? The answer is that rigid distinctions are unwarranted and that whatever assists the church (talents and fruits) is given by God—that is, is a gift from God—and should be accepted as a gift. Thus, love is both a fruit (Gal. 5:22) and a gift (1 Cor. 13).

Another question is whether some gifts are more and some less important. The answer, once again, is clear once one realizes that a gift is a skill given to a believer to be used to build up the church. Some skills build up the church better than others. Tongues and their interpretation, for example, do not so clearly build up the church and may actually damage the church.

If gifts are of different values, which is the most precious? It is one which, to the surprise of many, is available to all Christians. It is the one which Jesus declared to be the fulfillment of all the law and the prophets (Matt. 22:39-40). It is the gift of love (1 Cor. 12:31 to 13:13). Without it, all other gifts are useless. With it, the presence or absence of the other gifts is a matter of little concern. Love makes the new community possible. It guarantees that the other gifts will be used unselfishly, for the church, and not to enhance oneself. Love is the ultimate gift from God who is love.

STEWARDSHIP. The management of one's abilities, time, and resources for God, who is the Creator and Owner of all things.

A steward was a manager who administered the affairs of his owner or employer (Gen. 43:19; Matt. 20:8). Several of Jesus' parables were about stewards, some of farms and some of households. Paul referred to the leaders of the church as stewards, those who are entrusted with the safekeeping of the gospel (1 Cor. 4:1-2). In 1 Peter 4:10 all Christians are admonished to be good stewards of God's grace.

In the contemporary church, stewardship is often associated with financial contributions to the church; stewardship emphasis is understood to mean a financial emphasis. This idea of stewardship can be be enlarged through reflection and practice. To be a good steward entails using all that one has for the service of God. Stewardship emphases, which are biblical, will encourage Christians to be good managers of their resources as a result of what Christ has done for them (Phil. 2:1-11).

SUFFERING. The painful manifestation of sin in the lives of human beings.

Suffering in the Old Testament is understood as a punishment from God (Ezek. 18:2-4). Suffering is the theme of the Book of Job: how can we understand the unjustified suffering of the innocent? The answer of Job is that God is gracious and will set things right in the end (Job 42).

This solution became increasingly difficult to the Jews who did not believe in an afterlife and who did not always see the righteous vindicated in the present life. God led them to an understanding of an afterlife where restitution could be made for undeserved suffering.

In the New Testament, suffering is understood to be a part of human experience. It can be made meaningful to Christians who trust in God to take the suffering and use it to make them better people (1 Pet. 1:6-7). The pattern for this suffering is the suffering of Jesus on the cross (Heb. 13:12).

The New Testament teaches that suffering may come as a result of sin (Gal. 6:7). Jesus made it clear, however, that all suffering is not a direct result of personal sin (Luke 13:1-5). The final alleviation of suffering will take place when the kingdom of God is finally established (John 16:20-24). In the meantime, Christians must follow Jesus' example and do what they can to assist those who suffer unjustly (John 9:1-7).

T

TEMPTATION. Enticement to sin.

The first temptation recorded in the Bible was that of Adam and Eve in the Garden of Eden. Temptation sometimes might be understood as a test of one's faith. The New Testament affirms that God does not tempt anyone (Jas. 1:13). Temptation is understood by Christians as a part of being human. We live in a world in which we will be enticed to be disobedient to God.

God understands our condition since Jesus himself experienced temptation in the same way we do (Heb. 4:15). His greatest temptation took place in the wilderness where he was tempted to be selfish, self-centered, and disobedient. Because he was victorious over temptation, he was able to win a victory over sin on the cross. He proved that it was possible for a man to live a sinless life and to die an unjustified death without losing faith in God.

Jesus taught his disciples to pray that they would not be led into temptation (Matt. 6:13). By this he meant that they and we would pray that we will not be led into situations where we will be tempted. The power to overcome temptation is available to every Christian. It is the presence of Christ in the Christian's life. God has promised that this power is sufficient to meet any temptation to which one may be subjected (1 Cor. 10:13).

THEOLOGY. Thinking about God.

God takes the initiative in all his relationships with people. He acts, and people then respond to him. Human responses to God take a variety of forms. Some obvious ones are: faith, obedience, love, worship, missions, evangelism, prayer, ministry, preaching, singing, building churches, organizing programs, sponsoring institutions, writing music, painting and sculpting Christian art, writing books, and thinking about God. Thinking about God is a response which human beings make to God. It is not the most important response; love, prayer, and worship, for examples, are more important responses to God than thinking about God. But there is a place for thinking about God, or theology; it is a worthy response to God, and it can be of service to the church. When we think about God, we are loving God with our minds (Matt. 22:37).

Christians are not the only people who think about God. Jews do, and so do Moslems, Buddhists, Hindus, and even agnostics. In that sense, these people do theology. Theology is Christian when it is done by one who believes in Christ as the ultimate revelation of God. In this essay we shall be talking about Christian theology.

A distinction should be made between commonly held theology and the formal study of theology. All Christians have a theology; that is, they have their thoughts about the God whom they trust and worship. They may not articulate their thoughts very well, and they may not even like books and sermons about theology, but they have a theology nevertheless. Their theology should be treated with great respect, for it is a part of their authentic response to God.

There is also a formal study called theology. Like other disciplines, it has a history, with major figures, (such as Barth, Brunner, Tillich), moments of crisis, (Nicea, the Reformation), important books, and so on. It has a formal vocabulary, *(supralapsarian, realized eschatology)*, just as other disciplines do. It has its own methodology. It is divided into subdisciplines (Old Testament theology, New Testament theology, historical theology, apologetic theology, systematic theology, theological ethics, and so on). Professional theologians usually, but not always, see themselves as servants of the church. When they do, they often accept a Latin phrase from the writings of St. Anselm as descriptive of their work: *fides quaerens intellectum,* faith seeking understanding.

Even when they agree on a definition like this, they do not always agree with one another. Argument is a built-in component of the theological enterprise. In medieval universities, such as Paris and Oxford, students were required to debate publicly on an assigned theological concept in order to receive their degrees. All too often theological debates have been acrimonious; the reformer Melanchthon longed for death so that he could escape "the wrath of the theologians." Even today some Christians feel that they are obliged to act with hostility toward those whose theology differs from their own. The solution to this attitude is, first, to accept with humility one's own limitations and then to revise one's understanding of theology, thinking of it not as a competitive squabble but as a collegial activity in which fellow Christians who respect one another work together to try to grow in their understanding of God. Sometimes they may disagree, but the important thing is that they are together humbly seeking to love God with all their minds.

TRADITION. Teachings and practices passed down from generation to generation.

All institutions and communities develop traditions over time. This is true of the Christian church. The attitude of the church toward a tradition is ambivalent. On the one hand, the church wants to be free from the oppression of a dead and deadening past. Jesus illustrated this attitude when he rejected the traditions of the rabbis on matters, such as sabbath observance; Luther exemplified it when he rejected the oppressive traditions, such as indulgences, that had grown up in the Roman Catholic Church.

On the other hand, the church has a healthy respect for the traditions handed down from the past. It honors its fathers and mothers, recognizing that tradition is the accummulated wisdom of God's people over the centuries. Paul exemplified respect for tradition when he urged the church at Thessalonica to hold on to traditional teachings (2 Thess. 2:15) and practices (2 Thess. 3:6). He spoke of the gospel itself as something he had handed on (the word *tradition* means handed down) (1 Cor. 15:3), as indeed it was, in oral rather than written form, for twenty years (from the events of Jesus' death and resurrection to the first written Christian documents about AD 50).

Two other issues concerning tradition should be mentioned. The first is psychological. Some people are constituted so that they love the past; that is their psychological makeup. They are traditionalists, conservatives. Other people are constituted so that they love the new, the fresh; that is their psychological makeup. They are innovators, liberals. Conservatives who love Jesus think of him as the Savior who long ago died, the Lord whom the church has always worshiped. Liberals who love Jesus think of him as the Lord who awaits them in the future, who calls them on to an ever new adventure of life. It is inevitable that these attitudes will lead to disagreement. No one should be blamed for this, and there is no need for hostility. Actually, most people are partly conservative and partly innovative. God made human beings so that they can learn from the past and also so that they long to move into the future. And Jesus is, in reality, both the Savior who died long ago and the Lord who calls his church on into an open, unknown future.

The other issue concerns the relation of the Bible to Christian tradition. In the sixteenth century, the Reformers insisted that the Bible alone *(sola scriptura)* is authoritative for Christian faith and practice. The Roman Catholic Church replied at the Council of Trent that there are two sources of revelation, two authorities for Christian faith and practice: the Bible and the traditions of the Church. Today many Catholics do not defend this view, though it has not been officially renounced. However much Protestants respect tradition, they have stood by their conviction that it is subsidiary to Scripture and in fact must be judged in the light of Scripture. The Bible is a unique revelation of God, and tradition can never be more than a valuable witness to the teachings of Scripture.

TRINITY. God the Father, God the Son, God the Holy Spirit.

The understanding of God as Father, Son, and Holy Spirit is the most distinctive Christian belief about God. No other major world religion teaches that God is one and that God is also three. It is also a Christian teaching which has been officially approved by the church, articulated in its confessions of faith, defended by its theologians, and held by all except a tiny minority who, unless they were very uninformed, recognized that they were departing from traditional Christian teaching.

Yet, curiously, this universal and distinctive Christian belief, which is the subject of many books, many hymns, and much theological reflection, is not the subject of many sermons. How may this fact be explained? It probably is the result of an uneasiness which many Christians feel about the Trinity.

What are the sources of that uneasiness? There appear to be three principal sources. First, some Christians feel that the evidence for the Trinity is flimsy. Second, some Christians suspect that the doctrine of the Trinity may be self-contradictory. Finally, some Christians assume that the doctrine is not relevant to the practical concerns of Christian living and the ministry of the church. These issues will be dealt with in this essay.

Concerning evidence, it is true that the word *trinity* does not occur in the Bible (the word was invented by Tertullian in the second century, and it means tri-unity). It is also true that God has names other than Father, Son, and Holy Spirit. It is also true that no extended passage in the New Testament comprises a definition and discussion of the meaning of the Trinity. Is there then any biblical evidence in support of this understanding of God?

Indeed there is. First, God taught Israel that he was one God. The Jews were monotheists; the first Christians were all Jews. Next, God sent Jesus to save the world by his death and resurrection. What were the Christians to think of Jesus? They concluded that he was God, for the One who saves you is your God (an argument used repeatedly by Athanasius and other defenders of Jesus' deity). Finally, God sent his Spirit to the church, to guide and empower his people. How were the Christians to understand the Spirit? They knew him to be God.

The first level of evidence, then, is the historical. In the

Shema, Bethlehem, and Pentecost, God revealed himself as three The next level of evidence, which grew out of the history, was the experiential. The Jews experienced God as the one and only God; the disciples experienced Jesus as Emmanuel, God with us; and the church experienced the Spirit as God's presence in their lives.

First, the history. Second, the experience. The third level of evidence for the Trinity is the textual. Out of their trinitarian religious experience, the Christians wrote of Father, Son, and Holy Spirit, in passages such as Ephesians 1:3-14; 2:13-18; 3:1-6, 14-19; 4:4-6; 5:18-20. These passages are quite natural for those who had experienced what they had experienced, but they are very strange for Jewish monotheists. Yet, the early Christians remained true monotheists. There is not a shred of evidence to suggest that they ever challenged the view that God is one. But their monotheism was enriched, deepened by the revelation which God had given in Christ and at Pentecost. God was one, but he was not single; he was a complex, mysterious one, a unity of Father, Son, and Holy Spirit. The evidence, as thus construed, surely permits and probably requires a Trinitarian understanding of God.

The second source of uneasiness concerning the Trinity concerns its reasonableness. Is it reasonable to say that God is both one and three, or is it really a contradiction in terms, like saying that a circle can be drawn to have three sides and still remain a circle? Over the centuries the church has attempted to defend the reasonableness of its Trinitarian belief in various ways. The modern defense usually speaks of God as being like one person who is nevertheless made up of three components such as mind, emotions, and will, or else of saying that God is like three persons who are bound together in a unity of love so strong that it is appropriate to speak of them as somehow one. These are called the psychological and social analogies, respectively. Both have been considered acceptable by the church in the past. Neither one can prove the doctrine, but they are not used for that purpose; what they do is to show that it is not always nonsense to speak of a reality that is both one and three.

The third question concerns the relevance of the doctrine to the practical concerns of life. The Trinity is, in fact, a summary of Christian theology. It tells of one God who invades our world as Jesus Christ to provide salvation and who is present in the ongoing life of his people. A Christianity which fails to affirm all this is a poor substitute for a Trinitarian Christianity. Thus, a Christianity which does not affirm that there is a transcendent, personal God, is not even a religious faith. Again, a Christianity which does not affirm that Jesus Christ is God acting to save us is not really Christian at all. And a Christianity which affirms Father and Son but fails to affirm the Spirit leaves the church alone in the world to do its best and find its own way, which is hardly the traditional experience of the church. In brief, the understanding of God as Father, Son, and Spirit, is indispensable to a robust Christian faith in God and thus relevant to all of Christian and church life.

VIRGIN BIRTH OF CHRIST. The conception and birth of Jesus Christ, through the power of the Holy Spirit, through Mary the mother of Jesus, without benefit of sexual intercourse.

The virgin birth should be distinguished from simple parthenogenesis, which is the natural birth of a child to a mother who is a virgin, brought about by some unusual genetic occurrence. The conception and birth of Jesus was a supernatural event precipitated by God. The virgin birth affirms Jesus' humanity because it acknowledges that he had a human mother. It also affirms his divinity by its emphasis that God was Jesus' father. For this reason it is sometimes used as an equivalent to saying that Jesus was God incarnate.

The teaching concerning the virgin birth is found in Luke 1:28-35 and in Matthew 1:18-25. Paul did not mention it (but see Gal 4:4), and it does not occur in any of the sermons recorded in

Acts. It is, therefore, part of the church's theological teaching (*didache*), rather than of the church's evangelistic preaching (*kerygma*).

WILL OF GOD. God's purpose. The phrase is used in four distinct senses.

First, the will of God is God's overarching purpose in creation. Paul alluded to this (Eph. 1:7-10; 3:5-13), and it may be described as the creation of a community of persons of all races who freely choose to become God's people through faith in his Son, Jesus Christ, and who then love God and one another and thereby glorify God.

Second, the will of God is God's purpose for humanity's moral behavior. The Bible presents this in the form of commands, such as the Ten Commandments given to Israel (Deut. 5:6-21), the moral teachings of the Sermon on the Mount (Matt. 6:19 to 7:14), and Paul's instructions to churches (as, Rom. 12:9-21). For a Christian, right conduct is important not because it leads to a happy life or to a good society but because it is the will of God. Morality is obedience to the will of the righteous creator God.

Jesus taught that the divine commands are all summarized in the two commands to love God and neighbor (Matt. 22:34-40). Thus the goal of the biblical commandments is that people love God and their fellowmen. Legalism, which is keeping the letter but not the spirit of a law, is avoided by realizing that the divine commands are instructions about how love is to be put into action.

Third, the will of God is God's hidden purpose in tragedy. In the face of a tragedy which makes no sense at all, a faithful Christian may say, "It must have been the will of God." If this statement is taken literally it is untrue, for God is a God of goodness and love, not of evil; he does good and not evil. He can bring good out of evil, which is redemption, but evil itself is never his will but a violation of it.

However, if the statement is really a confession of faith, it should be understood to mean: "In spite of this tragedy, I believe that God is still in charge and can be trusted, and I trust him." This is a wonderful example of Christian faith and should be appreciated as such.

Fourth, the will of God is God's specific purpose for the life of an individual. For example, it was God's will for Paul to be an apostle (Rom. 1:1). The New Testament teaches that God assigns special tasks to certain individual Christians. While it does not go so far as to say that God has a blueprint for every detail of the life of every individual, many Christians have felt themselves led by God as they made decisions concerning important issues, such as marriage, family, and vocation.

Many of the questions concerning God's will are less puzzling when it is recognized that the phrase is used in the four distinct senses given.

WORSHIP. The loyalty, gratitude, reverence, adoration, and love which people have for God.

In the widest sense, man's worship of God may be expressed in many forms, including moral conduct and formal services of worship. In the narrower sense, worship is expressed in words, usually sung or prayed, and in gestures, such as kneeling and closing one's eyes, directed toward God.

Worship is practiced by virtually all religions, and a sense of awe and wonder toward the transcendent being or beings is almost universal. Even in the secular West in the twentieth century, the impulse to worship continues to be felt by many people. In view of these facts, it seems reasonable to assume that a deep instinct for worship exists in all people.

Worship is Christian when it is offered by persons whose understanding of God is that his deepest revelation of himself was given in Jesus Christ. The Christian faith teaches that when a person worships God, God is present and is actively meeting that person's deepest spiritual needs.

Varieties of Christian worship exist. Worship may be private or corporate, formal or informal, traditional or innovative. All have proved to have their place in the church. The important thing is that the community of faith truly adore God and that the forms of worship enhance that end, not displace it.

One form of Christian worship which was commanded by Christ and which has been observed by the church from its very beginning is the Lord's Supper (see Matt. 26:26-29; Acts 2:42).

Worship of God and service to people are closely related. Many Christians report that worship motivates and prepares them for service, and some have suggested that service is the test of the authenticity of worship.